JOHN
WHAITE
BAKES

JOHN WHAITE BAKES
RECIPES FOR EVERY DAY AND EVERY MOOD

headline

To my grandfather Merrick who taught me that the hungry dog hunts best. x

First published in 2013
by HEADLINE PUBLISHING GROUP

1

Cataloguing in Publication Data is available from
the British Library

Hardback ISBN 978 0 7553 6509 8

Project Editor: Mari Roberts
Design and Art Direction: Smith & Gilmour Ltd
Photography: Matt Russell
Food Stylist: Richard Harris
Typeset in Scala and Alternate Gothic
Printed and bound in Italy by Rotolito Lombarda S.p.A

HEADLINE PUBLISHING GROUP
An Hachette UK Company
338 Euston Road, London NW1 3BH
www.headline.co.uk

INTRODUCTION

When I was a little boy, my parents divorced. While this is no major sob story or catastrophic disaster, it really did shake up my little world, and I can see why so many people never truly recover from such an upheaval. Thankfully, I was lucky enough to have a mother for whom we – my sisters and I – were of paramount importance in the whole situation.

Mum would always make time for us and that time would be spent, happily and calmly, in the kitchen. Plates might have been broken only hours before in that same kitchen, but for us everything would be swept away and it became our sanctuary. This is not to say my parents didn't keep us informed about the divorce – they did – but when it came to our time with either of them, the bitterness melted away like butter, and the atmosphere was always serene and calm.

My sisters and I would spend what felt like hours in that kitchen with Mum, baking treats such as crispy cakes and gingerbread men. That time together was of fundamental importance. It gave us all something to concentrate on, and something to think about besides the sad events that were unfolding around us. One particularly fond memory I have is of Mum in her apron, her hair scruffily, but perfectly, clipped back. I would stand on my baking chair watching, enthralled by the way she hulled the tops from fairy cakes – as though performing a dance – to fill the cakes with floppy, sweetened cream and sharp raspberry jam. Even though it was probably fairly slapdash – my mum is a seriously slapdash kind of girl – for me the cakes looked perfect, and their taste was simple but pure, like the tangible love Mum had for us.

Whenever I pick up a bag of flour or a dozen eggs, these memories come flooding back to me, and I remember that time when baking – and excuse the drama – really did protect us as children. Since then, baking has been an inherently comforting process for me, and I turn to it whenever I am feeling particularly blue or when I'm worried about something. That said, I also bake when I am ecstatically happy or bored or inspired because I really do believe that there are bakes for every single mood. I have also included some of my favourite cocktails in this book, because I love to celebrate no matter how I'm feeling.

I am unashamed to admit that I am a moody person. I don't mean that I sit there constantly grumpy and cursing the world, but I am not a person of a perpetually perky personality. Some days I won't feel like getting out of bed, and I have done, and do, battle depression. Other days, I feel elated and excitable, and drive my family mad with ideas for all the various projects I may be working on. What I have found, though, over the years, is that whether my mood is up, down, or at some indescribable place in the middle, I bake. I bake because it is a comfort blanket, and because it is a form of artistic expression for me. I always joke that I was born with two left hands – I can't paint; even drawing a circle is tricky for me – but inside of me, in the darkest recesses of my being, there is an artist screaming to get out. Baking, for me, is also an expression of that little fella.

Whenever I look back at the times when my whole family has been together for a celebration, there has always been a copious amount of baking involved, and to this day Mum still bakes those fairy cakes. When my granddad died just after I had finished filming for the Great British Bake Off, I baked. I baked because I didn't know what else I could do to support my mum and my family. So I did the thing that Mum had done for me throughout my life when I needed comfort, I made sure she was nourished. I believe that baking is nourishment. Not only in the physiological sense, but psychologically too – the process of baking itself is nourishment for the soul. I find that working my way through a recipe gives me the time to be calm.

Of course, there are also times when I bake simply because I am a greedy monster and need a slice of chocolate and cassis cake, or something equally indulgent. These recipes are as much about indulgence as they are about mood, and it's important that we all treat ourselves to something delicious and delectable every so often – though for me this really does mean every day. People seem to be amused by the fact that I bake every day, but it is just what I do. I am a baker and without this process I don't think I could cope with my own, erratic self. In whichever direction my life path may lead, I just know that it will be littered with cake crumbs.

Whatever your reason is for baking, be it mood managing, indulgence or fun, I sincerely hope that you enjoy these recipes. And I hope too that you will create many a happy memory, safe in your kitchen, covered in flour and eggs.

EGGS

All recipes in this book use large eggs unless otherwise stated. I like to buy free range, and, where possible, organic. When I go home to Mum's, the local farm shop sells white-shell eggs with vibrant and sunny yolks; perfect for custards.

BUTTER

As the son of dairy farmers, I am told off if I buy anything other than British butter! When baking cakes, I use salted butter, because I find it contains the perfect amount of salt to bring out the other flavours. If I'm baking something that has a delicate flavour, or a custard, I always use unsalted butter. I specify which butter I use in all these recipes.

MILK

I always use whole milk. It works better, it tastes better and it's better for you. (Like I said above, I am the son of dairy farmers, and I know what's what.) All these recipes were made with whole milk. If you can get extra creamy milk, so much the better.

PLAIN FLOUR

I use plain flour in a number of recipes, and especially so in pastry. It is important to get the best quality you can afford, and to use it within its use-by date. Spelt flour can be a very nice, if expensive, alternative.

SELF-RAISING FLOUR

Again, better quality gives a better flour, but also I find that the raising agent will be more reliable. Cheaper self-raising flours tend either to have too much raising agent, so that your bakes over-rise and sink again, or not enough so that they end up stodgy.

BREAD FLOUR

For bread, you need strong flour (aka 'bread flour'), which has the higher gluten content that you need for good structure in bread. In this book I have recipes that use both white and wholemeal strong flours. If you're going to invest in just one best-quality ingredient, make it your strong white flour, because it will make such a difference to your loaves.

YEAST

I always use fast-action yeast, which I buy in a small canister. You can also get it in sachets, which contain 7g, but many of my recipes use less than this. Weighing out the right amount of yeast is very important, which is why digital scales are so vital. Yeast also requires tepid (barely warm) liquid.

CASTER SUGAR

This is one of the baking fundamentals. I always have jars full of white and golden caster sugar. Golden caster sugar has a hint more flavour, colour and nourishment than white. I like the light tint it gives to meringues. You can use whichever you prefer in these recipes; sometimes I express my preference, but still it's up to you.

MUSCOVADO SUGAR

Muscovado sugar is made from pure sugarcane juice. I use both light and dark brown muscovado. Light brown muscovado adds a soft treacle tang to bakes; it is beautiful in cookies as it makes them extra gooey. Dark brown muscovado adds a more intense, rich treacle tone to bakes. It has nutritional elements and flavour notes that other sugars lack.

PUFF PASTRY

If you buy puff pastry, which is perfectly acceptable and very handy, try to get an 'all-butter' one. However, a rough puff pastry is easily made, so don't be deterred (see page 22).

SHORTCRUST PASTRY

This pastry is so easy to make yourself – see page 20.

FILO PASTRY

Yes, you can make this, but the shop-bought stuff is so very good that I don't bother. Remember to defrost it in advance of use.

FLAVOURINGS

Avoid 'essences' like the plague. These are artificial flavourings and make bakes taste synthetic. I always opt for 'extracts' because these have a truer flavour, and give a better quality to the overall taste. For vanilla, where possible, I like to use real vanilla pods, or at least vanilla bean paste, but a good extract is also worthwhile.

ORANGES AND LEMONS

If for zesting, make sure they are unwaxed. If you can only find waxed, then scrub them with a clean brush under hot water to remove the wax.

FROZEN FRUITS

These are handy to have in, especially seasonal berries, cherries and rhubarb. They are a little soggier when defrosted than their unfrozen cousins, and so are best used for making compotes, jams and coulis, or fruit pie filings.

SPOON MEASUREMENTS

It's important to be absolutely accurate with these.

1 tsp = 5ml   1 tbsp = 15ml

FAN OVENS

Many recipe books give temperatures for both conventional and fan ovens. I find that modern fan ovens are so well calibrated that I am able to bake my goods in a fan oven at the temperatures stipulated for conventional. If you feel, though, that your fan oven burns on the hot side, then reduce the temperatures given here by 5–10°C.

WHEN IS A CAKE DONE?

One of the best ways to tell is to listen to the cake. If it is making a gentle bubbling, crackling sound – I like to say the cake is singing – then it is a little too moist in the centre, and is still baking. When the bubbling recedes, the cake is ready.

The most common test is to insert a skewer into the centre of the cake. If this comes out clean, with no mixture adhering to it, then it's ready. But be careful: if you're baking a cake with a high content of ground almonds or oil or fruit, then the skewer will always come out that bit 'soggier' than a simple butter and flour cake, even though the cake is done.

WHEN IS BREAD DOUGH SUFFICIENTLY KNEADED?

Kneading dough is about stretching and pulling it, and so developing the gluten that gives the bread its structure. Exactly how you do this is up to you, so long as you are pulling and stretching the dough. You will notice the dough becomes smoother and more elastic as you knead it. It takes about 10 minutes to knead dough by hand. Here are a couple of good tests to help tell you if you've done enough kneading.

The window test Flour your fingers to prevent them sticking, then pull off a little piece of dough. Gently stretch the dough thinner and thinner. If you can get it so thin that you can see light through it and it doesn't snap, then it is ready. If not, continue kneading until you see the light.

The poke test Roll the dough into a tight ball and flour a finger. Gently press the finger into the dough. If the dough feels smooth and elastic, and the indentation fills again when your finger is removed, it's done.

I really do believe that the most important part of baking is the preparation. I once did a photo shoot where I was expected to bake a Swiss roll. I arrived at my destination, the make-up artist was present and poised, the photographer had his finger on the trigger, and the journalist's pen was inked and ready. What was missing, however, was the most essential piece of equipment of the day: the Swiss roll tin. I simply couldn't do without it and so the photographer had to trundle to the shops to find one. The moral of the story is that equipment in baking is essential, and so below I have listed the 'armoury' that I find myself relying on day in, day out.

DISPOSABLE PIPING BAGS

These are so darn handy. I buy rolls of 100 large blue bags and they seem to last me for a very long time. The reusable ones are so difficult to clean, and I never feel as though I get them quite clean enough.

SELECTION OF PIPING NOZZLES

The range of piping nozzles available is wide. A basic kit containing at least a large star nozzle, a 1cm and 2cm plain nozzle, and a number 2, is a great thing to own. These are usable with disposable piping bags. You can also snip the corner off the disposable bag and use it like that, though the result will be a little less accurate.

MEASURING SPOONS

No baker should be without a set of these. Their accuracy is so vital, especially for flavourings and raising agents.

DOUGH SCRAPER

This is a really cheap, but incredibly handy, piece of equipment. It is great for when kneading wetter doughs by hand, and also for cleaning the worktop after baking.

HEATPROOF MIXING BOWLS

I prefer metal bowls. They are heatproof and therefore perfect for melting chocolate in; a metal bowl also gives you better volume when whisking egg whites.

STRONG BAKING SHEETS

I opt for the anodized aluminium baking sheets because they are so strong, which means they can't flex annoyingly and threaten to upend your bakes. They can't be put into the dishwasher, but they simply need a quick wipe clean.

WHISKS

I cannot live without my whisks. I have a regular balloon whisk, a small sauce whisk, and everything in between.

LOOSE-BOTTOMED CAKE TINS

I buy the lighter, anodized aluminium tins. They ensure an even bake and are much less susceptible to dents and scrapes. They can't be put into the dishwasher, so do line them with baking paper. I have both round and square ones, ranging from 15–28cm/6–11 inches. I have also included recipes in this book that use a 20cm/8-inch savarin tin, a 35×12cm/14×5-inch tarte maison tin, and a heart-shaped cake tin. If you're a keen baker, then these are a lovely addition to your armoury.

MUFFIN AND BUN TINS

For most recipes I use the 12, deep-hole kind. Some recipes call for the shallower 12-hole bun tin (aka jam-tart tin), and this is great to have alongside the deeper muffin tray.

MADELEINE TINS

These are such cute little tins. I have mine leaning against my kitchen wall as decoration when it's not in use. I use the anodized aluminium range, not only because of its strength, but also because the heat of the metal ensures the grooves of the madeleines are perfectly browned. Having said that, silicone madeleine trays are acceptable if that's all you can find, and they are substantially cheaper, too.

1LB AND 2LB LOAF TINS

I love to make traditional loaves of bread, and so loaf tins are vital for me. For the metrically inclined, these are 450g and 900g tins.

CIRCULAR COOKIE CUTTERS

These are so handy, not only for making cookies, but also for cutting out pastry for lining tart tins. A stack of these is inexpensive and really very useful. I have ones that are fluted on one side, and smooth on the other.

PASTRY BRUSHES

I much prefer the traditional bristled pastry brush, as I find the silicone ones leave pools of glaze on top of bakes, which is a baker's nightmare. That said, any pastry brush is better than none at all.

SILICONE SPATULAS

I must have about 10 of these in a jar on my kitchen worktop. Because silicone is heatproof I can mix hot sauces with them, but they are also perfect for mixing cake batter and folding, not to mention getting batter out of a bowl without leaving a trace behind.

BAKING PAPER

This comes in both white and brown. I personally prefer the brown as it seems to be slightly more non-stick, which can be vital, for example when making macaron shells.

CLING FILM

A kitchen basic – have it.

GRATER

I have different graters for different jobs. For zesting I use a long, thin Microplane zester. These are fairly pricey, but last a long time if well cleaned and cared for. For cheese I have a selection of coarse to fine graters.

JUICER

For me, this is an essential. As a baker, I love to use fresh juice in my creations. I have one juicer with a little tray that collects the juice and strains it to get rid of any pips.

SUGAR/JAM THERMOMETER

I couldn't make Italian meringue without this. You can buy one fairly cheaply and it's a real kitchen necessity.

FREESTANDING ELECTRIC MIXER

This is well worth the investment if you are a keen baker. Yes, they are pricey, but believe me it will change your baking life. I use mine for cakes, bread, pastry, pretty much everything.

HAND-HELD ELECTRIC MIXER

This is a great tool for making cake mixture and whipping cream. If you can't bring yourself to part with your money for a larger, freestanding mixer, then do invest in a good quality, hand-held mixer.

FOOD PROCESSOR

I love my food processor and use it every day. Like the freestanding mixer, these can be pricey, but a good one will last you a long time, and they usually have long guarantees. I use a large, costly mixer that comes with a variety of attachments. I use it every day, and it is worth every penny.

WOODEN SPOONS

You can never have too many.

CERAMIC BAKING BEANS/DRIED BEANS/ UNCOOKED RICE

For blind-baking pastry cases, one of these is completely, unequivocally necessary. If you don't have ceramic beans and you use real dried beans or dried rice instead, remember to keep them for just this purpose.

PASTRY BLENDER

This tool, for cutting butter into pastry, is very useful. If you have extremely hot hands, or don't trust yourself to be gentle, this cuts the butter into flour, which is a necessary step for pastry, scones and soda bread.

ELECTRONIC WEIGHING SCALES

Scales are the most important equipment in the kitchen. I use a set that can weigh a single gram so that I can be absolutely precise when I need to be.

FLAN RINGS

These allow you to make really professional-looking tarts with very straight sides. I think 25cm/10 inches is about the right size to start with. You use them in conjunction with a baking sheet.

BLOWTORCH

To get a really good finish on your Italian meringues, this is a genius piece of equipment to have, and won't set you back too much either.

COCKTAIL SHAKER

OK, so this may make you feel like a 1990s barman, but because I've included cocktail recipes in this book it seemed right to add it here. If you can't be bothered buying one, use a jam jar with a tight-fitting lid.

CHAPTER ONE
SIMPLE ESSENTIALS

Some recipes are simply the bread and butter of baking. These are recipes I use over and over again, and they often form the basis of another recipe. Take my rough puff pastry, for example; I use this in a multitude of things, from *tarte tatin* to *tarte fine*. So rather than repeat the essential basics over and over, I thought it preferable to have them in one easy place. And that way you have them to hand when you are experimenting with your own recipes, too.

PASTRY-MAKING TIPS

I always used to buy pastry because I was so afraid my big fat warm hands wouldn't allow me to make my own. I was wrong. I now love making pastry and find it so simple. The key thing is to ensure the ingredients are cold and that you touch them as little as possible; a light but confident touch is key.

1 Use cold ingredients, straight from the fridge. This will compensate for hot hands, if you have them.

2 Make sure you do not overwork the dough. By this I mean don't knead or manipulate it too much. Doing so would activate the gluten in the flour and bind the pastry together making it tough, rather than the flaky, crumbly texture required. (It's the opposite to what you do in making bread. For bread, you want the gluten to be activated.)

3 Possibly the most important thing about pastry is to chill it after making it, for at least 30 minutes. This allows the gluten in the flour to relax, which makes the pastry less resistant to being rolled, and thus less likely to shrink away from the tin.

4 Roll out the pastry to fit the tin. It doesn't matter if you can't get the pastry über-thin, and besides, working with thin pastry, if you're not used to it, is a tricky business. Remember also to keep your worktop and rolling pin well floured, and move the pastry about to be extra sure it isn't sticking anywhere. If you're using flan rings, remember to have them ready on a baking sheet, as once you've lined them, you can't move them from the baking sheet.

5 When the pastry is the desired thickness/ size, roll it around your rolling pin, then unroll it gently and loosely into the tin you are using. Be careful not to touch the sides of the tin with the rolling pin, as this will tear the pastry. Press the pastry down into the base and sides of the tin, and into the grooves if the tin is fluted, then fold the surplus pastry over the edge (this will allow you to slice it off when the case is baked, for an even, professional-looking finish).

6 When you have lined the tin, prick the base all over with a fork, then place in the freezer for 20 minutes. Preheat the oven to 200°C/Gas 6 for a regular shortcrust pastry, or 180°C/Gas 4 for a rich sweet pastry. Place a baking sheet into the oven to heat up; this will help ensure a well-baked base.

7 Blind-baking: remove the pastry case from the freezer, line it well with foil or baking paper, then fill it with baking beans (you can use – and reuse – ceramic beans, dried beans or uncooked rice). Place in the oven, on the baking sheet, and bake for 12–15 minutes. Then remove the beans and foil or paper lining, and return the case to the oven for a further 12–15 minutes. For perfect results, glaze the pastry with beaten egg white and bake for a final minute – this creates a waterproof layer. Now your pastry case is ready to fill and bake. You can blind-bake the pastry case in advance. Keep it, cooled, in an airtight container in a cool, dry place; it will keep under these conditions for 2–3 days.

SHORTCRUST PASTRY

MAKES ABOUT 450G

250g plain flour
125g salted butter,
   in 1cm cubes
1 egg
Cold water

This is deliciously flaky and melts in the mouth. Perfect for sweet and savoury bakes.

1 Place the flour and butter into a bowl, and swiftly but gently rub the butter into the flour until the mixture resembles fine crumbs.

2 Beat the egg in a cup, then add to the flour along with a teaspoon of cold water. Using your hands, gently clump the mixture together. If necessary, add more water, a teaspoon at a time, until the mixture comes together well, then gently knead it, though only for a second.

3 Wrap in baking paper and chill in the fridge for at least 30 minutes before using.

TIP
If you have a food processor, simply put the flour and butter in that with a blade attachment, and blitz. Add the egg and a little water and blitz, adding more water a teaspoon at a time if necessary, until the dough comes together into a ball. Remove and knead and continue as above.

RICH SWEET SHORTCRUST PASTRY

MAKES ABOUT 500G

1 egg
125g caster sugar
  (I like to use golden)
1 tsp vanilla or
  almond extract
250g plain flour
125g salted butter,
  in 1cm cubes

Essential equipment
Butter knife or
  pastry cutter

This is a beautiful, biscuit-like pastry, with a sweet flavour. It's so good, in fact, that I often make biscuits out of it, to devour. The amount of sugar in this pastry means it burns very easily, and so it is best cooked at a lower temperature.

1 Place the egg, sugar and extract in a mixing bowl, and whisk – I use a balloon whisk – for a minute, or until the sugar is dissolved into the egg.

2 Sift the flour into the mixture and stir in using a wooden spoon, until the mixture has a sandy texture – be sure to scrape around the bottom of the bowl so there are no clumps of flour.

3 Add the cubed butter, and cut in using a butter knife or a pastry cutter until the butter is well incorporated and the dough comes together. (This pastry gets too sticky too quickly to do this by hand, which is why you use a knife or cutter.) Remove from the bowl and knead gently for a few seconds. Wrap in baking paper and chill for at least 30 minutes before using.

ROUGH PUFF PASTRY

MAKES ABOUT 600G

250g plain flour,
  plus extra for dusting
250g salted butter,
  in 2cm cubes
1 tsp lemon juice
125–150ml cold water

Essential equipment
Rolling pin
Pastry brush

Making your own puff pastry is rewarding: it's lovely to see something so professional and know you created it yourself. Regular puff takes a while to master, but rough puff gives just as good an abundance of layers and takes less than half the time. If you think your hands might be too hot, just put your ingredients in the fridge 30 minutes before starting. The lemon juice in the recipe isn't for flavour; it helps to break down the gluten so the pastry doesn't go tough through all the working it gets. It also allows you to freeze the pastry for up to three months, well wrapped in baking paper, without it going a funny colour. Use offcuts by piling them on top of one another and re-rolling – never ball layered pastry up.

1 Put the flour and butter in a large mixing bowl and gently rub some of the butter through the flour – you still need large chunks of butter.

2 Stir the lemon juice into the water, then add to the flour, a little at a time, using your hands to bring the ingredients together. Tip out on to the worktop and lightly press and roll the pastry into a scraggy ball.

3 Flour the worktop and rolling pin. Roll the pastry out into a long thin rectangle – about 12cm/5 inches wide, and as long as it becomes when about 1cm thick. Brush excess flour from the pastry. Fold the two ends so they meet in the centre; brush excess flour off, then fold these doubled-up ends together like a book (this is called the 'book fold'.) Turn the dough a quarter turn and roll it away from you into a long rectangle again. Fold again as above, then wrap in baking paper and chill in the fridge for 15 minutes.

4 Remove from the fridge, repeat the rolling and book fold twice, making sure always to start with the folded edges of the pastry vertical, and to roll away from you. Then chill the pastry until you need to use it.

CHOUX PASTRY

MAKES ABOUT 600G

220ml water
80g butter
Pinch of salt
Generous pinch of sugar
125g plain flour
220g beaten egg

Ingredients for ²/₃ quantity
145ml water
55g butter
Pinch of salt
Pinch of sugar
85g flour
145g beaten egg

Ingredients for ¹/₃ quantity
75ml water
27g butter
Small pinch of salt
Small pinch of sugar
42g flour
75g beaten egg

Choux pastry is one of my favourite pastries to make. It is easy to do, and gives very impressive results. Some of the recipes in this book call for the full amount of the pastry, but others call for two-thirds or a third, and these quantities are given separately.

1 In a medium saucepan, gently heat the water, butter, salt and sugar until just boiling and the butter has melted.

2 Pour in the flour and beat vigorously with a wooden spoon until the paste is smooth and comes away from the sides. This should be done over the heat, but make sure you keep the paste moving so it doesn't burn. Decant into a cold bowl, and allow to cool for about 5 minutes.

3 Add the beaten egg, a little at a time, and incorporate well. This does take a while, and the mixture may look split at first but, believe me, it will come together. You need to get the paste to 'dropping' consistency. That is, when you scoop up a large amount, it should drop back down into the bowl within 5 seconds.

4 When the pastry is ready, put it into a piping bag for use. It will not keep and should be used straightaway.

CREME PATISSIERE

MAKES ABOUT 850G

4 egg yolks
125g caster sugar
40g cornflour
500ml milk
1 vanilla pod, halved
  lengthways, or 1 tsp
  vanilla paste or extract
40g unsalted butter

The staple ingredient for most things French. This is a delicious thick custard, which is perfect for piping into éclairs. The trick with this is to ensure you keep stirring the custard as you heat it for the second time, and to do so quite vigorously.

1 Place the egg yolks and caster sugar in a mixing bowl and whisk until the sugar is dissolved and the mixture is slightly paler in colour.

2 Add the cornflour and whisk well so there are no lumps of flour left. Place the bowl on a folded, dampened tea towel in readiness for the next stage.

3 Put the milk in a medium saucepan along with the vanilla and place over a medium-high heat until just before the milk boils. Pour half this milk into the bowl with the eggs, whisking continuously as you do so; the dampened tea towel helps stop the bowl sliding around.

4 When the milk is well incorporated into the eggs, pour it all back into the remaining milk in the saucepan and return to a medium-high heat, whisking constantly until the mixture is bubbling gently and is thick enough to coat the back of the spoon, barely dripping off. This will take 3–4 minutes.

5 Remove from the heat, continue to whisk for a minute more, then add the butter, stirring until it is melted into the crème pâtissière. Remove the vanilla pod, if you used one. Pour the crème pâtissière into a bowl, allow to cool briefly, then cover the surface with cling film (to prevent a skin forming) and refrigerate until needed. Use within a week.

TIP
If you need to cool the crème pâtissière quickly, pour it on to a large plate to increase the surface area, then cover with cling film and put it in the fridge.

FLAVOURED SUGARS AND SYRUPS

Flavoured sugars not only make for a perfect gift when stored in a cute jar and tied with a bow, but they can also turn an ordinary recipe into something of a masterpiece. Make a litre jar of flavoured sugar, allow to infuse, then use and/or decant into smaller, pretty jars to make gifts. The syrups that follow are perfect for making cocktails (see pages 248–52). You can also make your own vanilla paste with discarded pods and a little sugar syrup.

LAVENDER SUGAR

Put 900g sugar in a litre jar, add 2 tsp dried edible lavender flowers (available from most good supermarkets or online), close the lid, then shake it about. Leave to infuse for at least a month before using. This sugar is used for the Lavender and Raspberry Victoria Sponge recipe on page 71, but would also be great to replace the caster sugar in any shortbread recipe.

VANILLA SUGAR

As above, but with 1 vanilla pod split lengthways instead of the lavender. Great in most sweet recipes, and especially for making meringues. Remember to remove bits of pod from the sugar you are using in a recipe and return them to the jar.

LEMON SUGAR

As above, but add the zest of 2 lemons to the sugar. You could use this in the Lemon Meringue Cake on page 107, or the Lemon and Poppy Seed Scones on page 127.

SPICED SUGAR

As above, but this time using 1 star anise, 1 cinnamon stick, 3 bruised cardamom pods and 1 vanilla pod split lengthways. Lovely in the barley pudding on page 42.

SIMPLE SUGAR SYRUP

Boil 100g caster sugar with 100ml water for a few minutes, or until syrupy. Store in a clean jar.

LAVENDER SYRUP

Make sugar syrup as above, with the addition of 2 tbsp dried edible lavender. Strain, then store in a clean jar.

VANILLA PASTE

If you like to get your vanilla from real pods, as I do, then you will end up with a lot of pods too lovely to throw away. Do as I do and make your own vanilla paste: make a sugar syrup from 50g sugar and 50ml water, add 5 or 6 scraped vanilla pods and blitz into a paste in a food processor. It takes a little while to make a proper paste: keep scraping down and blitzing. Keep in a small jar in the fridge.

PASSIONFRUIT CURD

Pulp of 12 passionfruit
150g caster sugar
2 whole eggs and 3 egg yolks
125g unsalted butter,
  melted and cooled

Essential equipment
500g clean jam jar and lid,
  sterilized by being put
  into an oven at 180°C/
  Gas 4 for 20 minutes,
  then allowed to cool

This is my favourite curd. The exoticism of passionfruit is so good with the creamy, sweet texture of curd. This is perfect for my Tropical Sponge Pudding (see page 122), but I adore this just as much spread on toast. Store in a sterilized jar, in the fridge.

1 Put the passionfruit pulp into a food processor and blitz to loosen the seeds from the pulp.

2 Strain the passionfruit juice into a medium saucepan, and whisk in the sugar, eggs, egg yolks and butter. Set the pan over a medium heat and whisk constantly until the curd has thickened.

3 Remove from the heat and pour into a cold bowl. Cover with cling film and refrigerate until cold, then decant into the sterilized jar and store in the fridge.

LEMON CURD
As above, but substitute the zest and juice of 4 unwaxed lemons for the passionfruit juice, and start from step 2.

CHAPTER TWO
SEEKING SWEET SOLACE

When I started at Oxford University, where I'd gone to study Italian, I suffered a serious bout of depression, and it was truly impossible for me to perk up. I had to find salvation and solace, and I did that through baking. The baking allowed me time to collect my thoughts, and to come to the realization that the only option for me was to go home. I think the meditative and therapeutic nature of working through a recipe and creating something is a godsend, and it was certainly one that helped me make a fundamental life decision.

Even now that I am free from the confines of doing something I didn't want to do, I still have days when I just feel blue, as I'm sure most people do. The recipes here are ones I have created on such days, and they help lift me up.

THE LONE WOLF'S BAKED EGGS

INGREDIENTS PER PERSON

Butter for greasing
2 eggs
30ml cream or milk
A few leaves of thyme
   (optional)
Pinch of salt and pepper
A good grating of a
   cheese of your choice
   (I use a strong Cheddar)

When I was a teenager, my mum used to say that I was a 'lone wolf' because I wasn't particularly fond of being around people all the time. To this day, while I love my family and friends dearly, there are certain times when I just long to be 'tutto solo', and when I do get time alone, I bake these eggs, snuggle down under my duvet, and dip sourdough or freshly baked focaccia into the little beauties.

1 Preheat the oven to 170°C/Gas 3.

2 Grease a short fat teacup or ramekin with butter and break the eggs into it; do not break the yolks. Gently pour on the cream or milk, and sprinkle with thyme, salt and pepper, then put the grated cheese on top. Don't stir anything.

3 Place the cup or ramekin on a baking sheet and bake for 12–14 minutes, so that the white is just set, and the yolk is perfectly runny.

OVERNIGHT RUSTIC FRENCH BAGUETTE
MAKES 4

For the ferment
100g wholemeal bread flour
5g fast-action yeast
150ml tepid water

For the dough
400g white bread flour
10g salt
5g fast-action yeast
200–220ml tepid water
Wholemeal bread flour
   for dusting

Essential equipment
Dough scraper
4 baking sheets
Spray bottle filled with water

In moments of romantic melancholy I like to imagine myself in an old black and white film, walking down a Parisian street, snacking on a freshly baked baguette. That is why I decided to include a recipe for these here in the solace chapter. That, plus the fact that the smell of these baking will take your mind off whatever is bothering you. The first stage of this process is to make a ferment, or starter, which is left for 24 hours to develop the flavour. Although that can sound daunting, trust me that it really couldn't be easier. What's more, I always think it gives me a little 'creature' to take care of, which works wonders for remedying a blue mood.

1 Make the ferment by putting the flour into a mixing bowl, stirring the yeast through, then adding the water and mixing to a thick paste. Cover with a towel or cling film, and leave for no less than 24 hours.

2 When the ferment has been resting for 24 hours, start the dough. Place the flour in another mixing bowl and stir the salt through it. Then add the yeast and stir through. Using a dough scraper, scrape the ferment into the bowl, and add 200ml water. Mix together to a sticky, fairly wet dough; you may need an extra 10–20ml water to get the right consistency.

CONTINUED OVERLEAF

OVERNIGHT RUSTIC FRENCH BAGUETTE CONTINUED

3 Tip the contents of the bowl out on to the counter top and knead until the dough is smooth and elastic: this usually takes around 10 minutes. When the dough is ready, place in a clean, floured bowl, and cover with a cloth to rise for 1 hour. If you prefer, knead the dough in an electric mixer with dough hook for about 5 minutes.

4 Place a clean tea towel on the counter top and dust it liberally with wholemeal bread flour. After the dough has risen for an hour, gently scrape it out of the bowl using a dough scraper, trying not to deflate it, and place it on the counter. Using a sharp knife or the dough scraper, cut the ball of dough into quarters. Roll each quarter into a sausage shape, about the length of the tea towel's width. Place the dough sausages on to the floured tea towel, with pleats in between to prevent them touching. Cover with another tea towel and allow to rise for 45–60 minutes.

5 Preheat the oven to 230°C/Gas 8, and put 2 baking sheets in to heat up. Flour 2 other baking sheets well.

6 Bake the baguettes 2 at a time. Place one on each of the well-floured baking sheets. With a sharp knife, slash across the top of each baguette at an angle – I get about 5 or 6 slashes on this size of bread – then slide each baguette on its baking sheet directly on to the hot sheets in the oven. Before shutting the oven door, quickly spray a mist of water inside. This water will help to create a great crust on the baguettes. Bake for 12–15 minutes.

FRENCHIFIED FRENCH TOAST

INGREDIENTS PER SERVING

60ml milk
1 egg
Few drops of vanilla extract
2 stale croissants or
  pains au chocolat
Sunflower oil for frying
Caster sugar and lemon
  juice, to serve

I love French toast. It is the perfect quick fix when I wake up on the wrong side of the bed. It is wonderful with honey, maple syrup or blueberry sauce, but I prefer mine just rolled in caster sugar, with a gentle spritz of lemon juice. That simplicity, but that taste, is just a giant cuddle on a plate. Make sure you use properly stale croissants or pains au chocolat.

1 Beat the milk and egg together in a bowl with the vanilla extract. Drown the croissants in this mixture, and leave to soak for just a minute or two – you don't want them to be too soggy.

2 Heat a little oil in a frying pan over a high heat until smoking hot, then reduce the heat to medium-high.

3 Remove the croissants from the soaking liquid, allowing excess to drip off, and place them in the frying pan. Fry on each side for about 1 minute, or until perfectly golden and crisp on the outside, with a fluffy, custardy inside. Roll in caster sugar, squeeze over some lemon juice and eat at once.

CARAMELIZED ONION AND ROSEMARY FOUGASSE
MAKES 4

1 red onion
Knob of salted butter
1 tsp balsamic vinegar
1 tsp caster sugar
500g white bread flour
10g salt
7g fast-action yeast (1 sachet)
2–3 sprigs of rosemary,
    finely chopped (or herb
    of your choice)
350ml tepid water
Wholemeal bread flour
    for dusting

Essential equipment
Dough scraper
4 baking sheets
Spray bottle filled with water

This is simply beautiful. I could eat, and have eaten, a whole batch of these as soon as they come steaming out of the oven. The amount of rosemary you put in is entirely up to you. You might even prefer to use a different herb; thyme or parsley would work a treat.

1 Peel and finely slice the onion. Melt the butter in a frying pan over a high heat, then add the onion. Immediately turn the heat down to low-medium and cover the pan with a lid. Allow the onion to cook gently for 15 minutes, then add the vinegar and sugar and cook for a further 5 minutes on a low heat, this time uncovered. Remove from the heat and allow to cool completely.

2 To make the dough, place the flour in a mixing bowl and stir the salt through it. Then stir in the yeast and chopped rosemary. Add the water in thirds, and bring the dough together into a sticky mass.

3 Tip the contents of the bowl out on to the counter top and knead for about 10 minutes. Then incorporate the onions, kneading for a few more minutes until they are evenly distributed and the dough is smooth and elastic. Place in a clean, floured bowl. Cover the bowl with cling film and leave to rise for 1 hour or until the dough has doubled in size.

4 Dust 2 of the baking sheets liberally with wholemeal bread flour, and dust your counter top, too. Gently tip the risen dough out on to the counter, using a dough scraper to help remove it from the bowl. When the mound of dough is on the counter, cut it into quarters using a sharp knife or dough scraper. You should then have 4 portions of dough, shaped like rounded triangles or leaves.

5 Take one portion of dough and, using the thin edge of the dough scraper, cut a line in the middle from the tip of the triangle to the flat edge. You are cutting right through the depth of the dough, but not to each end, because you do not want to cut the dough in half: there needs to be 2cm dough uncut at either end of the line. This line will be like a centre vein on a leaf. Then, on either side of that line, at a 45 degree angle, cut three little 'veins' in the same way. Stretch the dough slightly so the holes open up. Repeat with the other 3 pieces of dough. (See the photograph overleaf.)Place 2 leaves on each floured baking sheet. Allow to prove for 30 minutes more.

6 Preheat the oven to 230°C/Gas 8. Place the other 2 baking sheets in to heat up.

7 Slide the breads on their baking sheets directly on to the hot sheets in the oven, spraying a mist of water inside before you shut the door. Bake for 12–15 minutes.

CHERRY AND CLEMENTINE TART
SERVES 8–12

1 quantity Shortcrust Pastry
(see page 20)
800g pitted fresh cherries
250g light brown
muscovado sugar
Zest of 2 large clementines
or tangerines
Ice cream of your choice,
to serve

Essential equipment
25cm/10-inch loose-
bottomed flan tin or flan
ring on a baking sheet

Whenever I'm being a grump and making my family's life difficult, this is one of the bakes that can really sort me out. The pastry for this tart isn't blind-baked; I like to eat this dessert just baked with still soft pastry and lashings of ice cream.

1 Preheat the oven to 200°C/Gas 6.

2 Roll out the pastry to about 3mm thick and use it to line a 25cm flan ring on a baking sheet (if you don't have a flan ring you could use a 25cm loose-bottomed flan tin, but then you would have leftover filling because a tin is shallower than a ring). Press the pastry into the corners of the ring and fold the excess pastry tightly over the edges – you will cut this off after the tart is baked. Put the pastry case into the fridge for 20 minutes.

3 Place the cherries in a mixing bowl and add the sugar and zest, mixing everything together. Scoop the cherry mixture into the uncooked pastry case and spread it out. Bake for 40–45 minutes until the excess pastry is heavily browned and the cherries have lost their plump form. Remove from the oven and trim off the excess pastry by running a sharp knife at a right angle along the rim.

4 Allow to cool completely, then refrigerate for at least 2 hours before eating – it will still be a fairly runny tart, but this, when you serve it with ice cream, makes for a delicious cherry ripple sauce.

A GIANT HUG IN A BARLEY-FILLED BOWL
SERVES 4–6

Butter for greasing
200g dried pearl barley
400ml double cream
700ml milk
100g light brown
   muscovado sugar
Zest of half an orange
Pinch of nutmeg
Seeds from 1 vanilla pod,
   or 1 tsp vanilla paste
   or extract
75g currants
30ml ginger wine

Essential equipment
Pudding dish (I use a 23cm/
   9-inch square ceramic dish)

I don't think there could be anything more comforting than this pudding. It truly is a giant hug in a bowl, and whenever I am feeling glum, this is sure to make me feel a whole lot better. This was originally a rice pudding. It was delicious, but the next time I wanted to make it I had only pearl barley in the cupboard – poor student days – and so I tried that. I'm pleased I did. The plump pearls are much more comforting and toothsome than rice, and now I only ever make it this way. I love to have ginger wine in the store cupboard; it's perfect for times like this, when a dish needs its gentle warming quality.

1 Preheat the oven to 150°C/Gas 2. Grease a pudding dish with butter.

2 Put the pearl barley in a sieve and rinse under cold water until the water runs clear, then transfer to the pudding dish.

3 Pour the cream and milk into a medium saucepan and bring just to the boil over a high heat, stirring constantly. Remove from the heat and stir in the sugar, orange zest, nutmeg and vanilla. Pour this over the barley in the pudding dish.

4 Bake the pudding for 90 minutes, stirring every 20 minutes or so. Meanwhile, put the currants in a cup and pour the ginger wine over them. Allow to soak until needed.

5 When the pudding is baked, the pearl barley should be soft and tender. Remove from the oven and pour in the currants and ginger wine. Best eaten from a bowl while tucked under a duvet on the couch.

MIDNIGHT BLUES TART
SERVES 6-8

1 quantity Crème Pâtissière
(see page 24)
Zest of 1 lemon
2 tsp Limoncello liqueur
(optional)
1 quantity Rich Sweet
Shortcrust Pastry
(see page 21)
2 leaves gelatine
350g frozen blueberries
Juice of 1 lemon
150g caster sugar
50g white chocolate
300g fresh blueberries
Edible gold stars
Edible glitter

Essential equipment
23cm/9-inch fluted tart tin
Pastry brush

I sometimes find myself craving something tart and crisp to cut through my grumpiness. What's more, creating something helps to lift me up, and this really is a creation: a tart with blueberry jelly and lemon crème pâtissière. I add edible gold stars and glitter to make it look like a midnight sky (see overleaf).

1 Make the crème pâtissière according to the recipe on page 24. Mix the lemon zest and Limoncello, if using, into it, cover and place in the fridge until set.

2 Make the pastry according to the recipe on page 21, line the tart tin, chill it, then blind-bake it as described on page 19. Set aside to cool.

3 Put the gelatine in a bowl of cold water to soak. Put the frozen blueberries, lemon juice and sugar in a saucepan over a high heat. Stir until the sauce begins to bubble, then reduce the heat and simmer for about 5 minutes or until slightly reduced and the blueberries have lost their shape. Remove from the heat. Take the gelatine leaves, which should now be floppy and yielding, squeeze the moisture from them and add them to the blueberry sauce. Stir until dissolved, then allow to cool for about 10 minutes.

4 Melt the white chocolate in a heatproof bowl set over a pan of simmering water. Use a pastry brush to paint the inside of the baked and cooled pastry case with it. Allow this to set for about 5 minutes. Spoon the crème pâtissière into the case and level it off.

5 Stir the fresh blueberries into the blueberry sauce and stir to coat them, but don't pop them. Gently spoon over the crème pâtissière. Finish the tart with gold stars and glitter, and allow the jelly to set for a few hours, or overnight, before serving.

BIG SUE'S TINY ORANGE NATAS
MAKES 24

1 quantity Rough Puff Pastry
 (see page 22) or 500g shop-
 bought all-butter puff pastry
½ quantity Crème Pâtissière
 (see page 24)
Zest of 1 small orange
1 tbsp Cointreau liqueur
Icing sugar for dusting
Butter for greasing

Essential equipment
7.5cm/3-inch cookie cutter
2×12-hole shallow bun tins,
 greased with butter

I love custard tart so much, but only recently did I discover this Portuguese version, made with sweetened and flaky puff pastry, filled with blistered custard. It was my brother-in-law's mum, Sue – or Big Sue, as we call her in jest – who told me about them, and ever since I first tried one I have been making them at least once a month. They are the perfect bite-sized treat for every mood, but I particularly crave these if I'm feeling under the weather. Normally they are made with crème anglaise, but on Richard Bertinet's recommendation I make mine with crème pâtissière, which I think gives a better textured nata. Natas are often made a little larger than in this recipe, but with the enrichment from the orange and liqueur, I find these are the perfect size.

1 Prepare the Rough Puff Pastry (see page 22) and put in the fridge to chill. Prepare the crème pâtissière as on page 24. Stir the orange zest and liqueur into the crème pâtissière, and allow to cool completely.

2 Preheat the oven to 220°C/Gas 7.

3 Sift a heavy covering of icing sugar on to the worktop and roll out the pastry to about 3mm thick. Cut out 24 circles using the cookie cutter. Line the greased bun tins with the pastry circles, and fill each one with a good blob of the cooled, orange-infused crème pâtissière – I do this using a piping bag to avoid spillages. Be sure not to fill them more than half full, because the crème pâtissière will rise as it bakes.

4 Place the natas in the hot oven and bake for 12–15 minutes, or until the pastry has puffed up and is a deep golden brown, and the crème pâtissière is slightly charred in areas. Watch carefully for the last 2 minutes to make sure they don't burn. Remove from the tins while hot, and allow to cool before serving.

SELF-SAUCING CHOCOLATE MUD PUD

SERVES 6–8

250g plump raisins
350ml boiling water
1 tsp bicarbonate of soda
60g salted butter,
   at room temperature
250g dark brown
   muscovado sugar
Seeds from 1 vanilla pod,
   or 1 tsp vanilla paste
   or extract
2 eggs
260g plain flour
50g cocoa powder

For the self-saucing sauce
2 tbsp cocoa powder
75g dark brown
   muscovado sugar
300ml boiling water
50g chocolate
   hazelnut spread

Essential equipment
Deep 23cm/9-inch
   square ceramic pudding
   dish, greased

If I'm feeling lonely, I seek out good company to dig into a pudding with me. This pudding is perfect for a catch-up. Even better, you don't need to bake the pudding and then bake it again with sauce – it sorts itself out. Very good served with whipped double cream.

1 Chop the raisins as finely as you can, and place them in the boiling water with the bicarbonate of soda. Allow to soak for 30 minutes.

2 Cream the butter with the sugar until paler in colour and lighter in texture (a freestanding mixer or an electric whisk is useful for this), then add the vanilla and the eggs. Beat together vigorously until everything is well combined, then add the raisins and their soaking water. Sift together the flour and the cocoa powder, and fold this into the batter.

3 Alternatively, if you have a food processor, simply soak the raisins as in step 1, then throw everything into the food processor and blitz into a chocolaty batter.

4 Pour into the greased dish, cover with cling film and place in the fridge to firm up for at least 2 hours. Preheat the oven to 160°C/Gas 3.

5 For the sauce, mix the cocoa powder and muscovado sugar together and sprinkle evenly over the pudding. Mix the boiling water and chocolate hazelnut spread together until well combined – best done with a whisk in a mixing bowl – and then gently pour on top of the pudding. Immediately place in the oven and bake for 45 minutes to 1 hour, or until the pudding is spongy and has risen slightly. Serve warm.

CHAPTER THREE
CALMING A BAG OF NERVES

Apprehension is something that affects us all at some point in our lives. I am a natural worrier. As a little boy I often had a horrible day dream that the world would split in half while I was at school. I would be on one half of the world and my family would be on the other half and these two halves would float around the universe entirely separate, never to reunite.

To this day, I still worry about the silliest of things – something that may or may not even happen – and I really don't think it helps that I am of an impatient disposition. I sometimes find that the only way I can take my mind off something is by taking myself off to the kitchen. The recipes in this chapter are ones that I have developed during times of panic, worry or impatience, and they have helped me to calm down.

WHOLESOME WHOLEMEAL LOAF
MAKES A LARGE LOAF

Stage 1
125g strong wholemeal flour
125ml tepid water
2g fast-action yeast

Stage 2
125g strong wholemeal flour
125ml tepid water
2g fast-action yeast

Stage 3
250g strong wholemeal flour
150ml tepid water
2g fast-action yeast
10g salt

Essential equipment
2lb (900g) loaf tin

A good wholemeal loaf is, for me, the epitome of comfort. Not only does it look and smell cosily warming, but with the high amounts of fibre I feel as though each slice nourishes my every cell. I decided to add this recipe to the chapter because not only does the process of kneading allow you to work your worries away, but the four-hour time frame also gives you something else to be thinking about. You mix stage 1, then, while you wait for an hour, you have stage 2 to think about and prepare for, and so on.

A 100% wholemeal loaf can be a tricky thing to get right. Sometimes the gluten is insufficiently developed, and the loaf's structure is dense. Fear not, because with my three-ferment method, I have found that you can get a really light, perfect wholemeal loaf.

STAGE 1: In a large mixing bowl, mix together the 'stage 1' ingredients with a spoon, and leave, uncovered, to rest for about 1 hour.

STAGE 2: To the 'stage 1' mixture add the 'stage 2' ingredients, mix as above, and leave to rest for 1 hour.

CONTINUED OVERLEAF

WHOLESOME WHOLEMEAL LOAF CONTINUED

STAGE 3: Now add the 'stage 3' ingredients, mix well, then knead for about 10 minutes by hand, or 5–6 minutes in a machine, until you have a smooth dough. This is a quite wet dough, but as I learned from Paul Hollywood, a wetter dough equals a better loaf. Leave the dough to prove, uncovered, for 1 hour, or until doubled in size.

FINAL STAGE: After the dough has doubled in size, knock it back by firmly prodding the surface of the dough, which will cause it to shrink in on itself. Roll into a fat sausage, the length of your 2lb loaf tin. Place it in the tin and allow to rise for between 30 minutes and 1 hour, or until doubled in size again. Meanwhile, preheat the oven to 230°C/Gas 8.

Bake the loaf in the hot oven for 25–30 minutes. Using oven gloves, tip the loaf out of the tin and tap it on the bottom to find out if it sounds hollow. If it does, it's done. If not, allow the loaf to fall back into the tin and give it a few minutes more. Cool, then slice into thick chunks, as I do, and slather it in salty butter.

PLAIT OF WORRIES LOAF

MAKES A LARGE LOAF

500g strong white flour
7g fast-action yeast (1 sachet)
10g salt
300ml tepid water
1 egg yolk beaten with a
   pinch of salt, for glazing

This is for my best friend, Holly. She is the funniest person I know. 'Plait of Worries' was the title track of the one-track album she and her girl-band created when they were 12. (How many worries can a 12-year-old really have?) The official reason for including this loaf is that the process of following the plaiting pattern can be very absorbing. Not only that, but when you see the bronzed beauty come steaming out of the oven, you will know you've done good.

1 Put the ingredients (except the egg yolk) in a bowl and bring together into a rough dough. Knead by hand for 10 minutes, or in a mixer with a dough hook for about 6, or until you have a smooth, elastic dough. Place in an oiled bowl and allow to rise for about an hour, or until doubled in size.

2 Turn the dough out, then divide into 6 equal balls (about 135g each). Roll these into long sausages of the same length (about 35cm). Press the dough sausages all together at one end, then begin the plait: starting on whichever side you feel like, take the outermost strand and place it under the next two, over the next one, then under the final two. Take the next outermost strand (always from the same side!) and repeat (see overleaf). Repeat until all the strands are tightly braided, and tuck the ends under to neaten them off. Leave the braided loaf to prove for about an hour. Preheat the oven to 230°C/Gas 8.

3 When the loaf has about doubled in size, glaze with the egg yolk. Bake for about 30 minutes, or until perfectly bronzed and hollow-sounding when tapped on the bottom. What were you worried about?

PERFECTION IN A PLAIN LOAF

MAKES A LARGE LOAF

500g strong white flour
10g salt
20g sugar
10g fast-action yeast
100ml milk
240ml tepid water
40g unsalted butter, melted
Vegetable oil

Essential equipment
2lb (900g) loaf tin

I find that not only does the process of weighing, kneading and proving help my anxiety, but the smell of this loaf also fills the kitchen with what can only be described as a giant, familiar cuddle.

1 Place the flour in a mixing bowl with the salt and sugar, and mix together. Add the yeast and mix through, then make a well in the centre. Mix the milk, water and butter in a jug, then pour half into the flour, mixing with a fork. Slowly add the remaining liquid, then squeeze the dough together for a minute in the bowl. Turn out on to the worktop and knead for 10 minutes, or until smooth and elastic. (Or knead in a mixer with a dough hook for 6 minutes.)

2 Place the dough in an oiled bowl, rolling it around to cover it with the oil, then cover the bowl with cling film. Set aside to rise for about 1 hour or until doubled in size.

3 Turn the dough out of the bowl, allowing it to deflate a little (this is 'knocking it back'), then roll into a sausage about the size of the loaf tin. Place in the tin, cover with cling film and set aside until doubled in size, which should take another hour.

4 Preheat the oven to 200°C/Gas 6. When the oven is hot and the dough is risen, bake it for 25–30 minutes, or until it sounds hollow when tipped out of the tin and tapped on the bottom.

NUTTY COOKIES
MAKES 24

150g salted butter,
   at room temperature
150g light brown
   muscovado sugar
80g almonds,
   roughly chopped
80g pecans,
   roughly chopped
1 egg
1 tbsp golden syrup
200g plain flour
1 tsp baking powder
1 tsp mixed spice

Essential equipment
2 baking sheets, lined
   with baking paper

Biscuits are, without doubt, a comforting treat. I think that if you feel in need of a helping hand, it is well worth rustling up a batch to boost your energy levels. That's my excuse anyway. Even more convincingly, nuts are rich in selenium and so make you happy on a chemical level too. However you analyse it, these nutty cookies will make you feel less nutty.

1 Preheat the oven to 190°C/Gas 5. In a large mixing bowl, cream together the butter and sugar until paler in colour and lighter in texture. This is easier with an electric whisk or in a freestanding mixer, but a wooden spoon and a bit of effort will do the job just as well. Add the nuts, egg and golden syrup and stir together. Sift in the flour, baking powder and spice, and bring together into a fairly stiff dough.

2 Divide the dough into 24 small balls of a size that would fit neatly into your palm. Or, if you are feeling really pedantic, weigh out 24 balls of about 30g each. If the dough is too sticky to handle, put it in the fridge for 10–20 minutes to firm up. Place the dough balls on 2 baking sheets – they need plenty of room to expand – and lightly press them down into cookie shapes.

3 Bake for 9–12 minutes, or until the edges are just starting to go golden and the underneaths are nicely browned. Remove from the oven and allow to cool down and firm up before gobbling up.

APRICOT AND WHITE CHOCOLATE FLAPJACKS
MAKES 16

200g dried apricots
225g salted butter, cubed
120g light brown
   muscovado sugar
150g runny honey
Zest of 1 lemon
2 tbsp treacle
400g rolled oats
200g white chocolate
   for topping

Essential equipment
30×20cm/12×8-inch Swiss
   roll tin, greased and lined
   with baking paper

There is something reassuring about knowing I always have the ingredients in my cupboard to throw together a batch of these chewy creatures. If I am feeling particularly anxious and need to sink my teeth into something alongside a good cup of coffee, I make these.

1 Preheat the oven to 180°C/Gas 4.

2 Finely chop the apricots. Put the butter, sugar and honey in a saucepan over a medium heat and stir until melted and well mixed, then add the apricots, lemon zest and treacle and mix in. Tip in the oats and stir into an oaty mush.

3 Dollop into the prepared tin and even out. Bake for 20–25 minutes, or until just darkened around the edges and golden brown in colour.

4 Remove from the oven and allow to cool completely before turning out from the tin and slicing into 16 rectangles or triangles.

5 Melt the white chocolate in a heatproof bowl over a pan of barely simmering water. From here you have a couple of choices. You can dunk one end of each flapjack into the melted chocolate, or you can drizzle the melted chocolate over the flapjacks. Or maybe do half and half. Allow the chocolate to set.

SIMPLE STRAWBERRY TART
SERVES 8

1 quantity Rich Sweet
  Shortcrust pastry
  (see page 21)
1 quantity Crème Pâtissière
  (see page 24)
700–800g strawberries
1 tbsp caster sugar
6 tbsp apricot jam

Essential equipment
23cm/9-inch loose-
  bottomed flan tin
Pastry brush

A classic strawberry tart – filled with pastry cream and topped with apricot-jam-glazed strawberries – is a thing of great beauty. I first made this tart a few nights before travelling down to Oxford University in order to try to calm myself. It is such a simple recipe, it really does give you time to think, to process information that's whizzing around in your head. The tart itself tastes so good you won't be worrying about anything else when you have a forkful.

1 Make the pastry according to the recipe on page 21. On a floured work surface and using a floured rolling pin, roll it out to a thickness of about 4mm and use it to line the tin. Chill in the fridge for 30 minutes, then blind-bake as described on page 19. Set aside to cool.

2 Make the crème pâtissière according to the recipe on page 24 and allow to cool completely.

3 Hull the strawberries by removing the green tops with a knife, and then slice each strawberry in half. Place in a bowl with the caster sugar and mix about gently so that each strawberry is covered in sugar. Set aside for the strawberries to macerate and go shiny.

4 Fill the cold pastry case with the crème patissière, and then top with the strawberries – you can make a neat pattern, or simply allow the strawberries to tumble over the surface.

5 Make a glaze: heat the apricot jam in a small saucepan then sieve it into a bowl. Use a pastry brush to paint the strawberry tops and any bare crème pâtissière with apricot glaze. Refrigerate until served.

PISTACHIO AND ROSEMARY BISCOTTI
MAKES 18–20

125g plain flour
75g caster sugar
½ tsp baking powder
Zest of 1 large orange
50g dried apricots,
   roughly chopped
80g pistachio kernels,
   roughly chopped
1 sprig rosemary,
   finely chopped
1 egg
1 tbsp milk

Essential equipment
Baking sheet

There's something very relaxing about the aromatic scent of rosemary. I adore it. These biscotti are perfect for nibbling when there is something on your mind, and especially good when you are drinking cappuccini, or maybe a shot of something stronger, with a friend.

1 Preheat the oven to 180°C/Gas 4. Place the flour, sugar, baking powder, orange zest, apricots, pistachios and rosemary in a mixing bowl and stir together so that everything is evenly dispersed.

2 Beat the egg with the milk, and then pour this into the bowl. Bring everything together into a dough. I find it easiest to use my hands: grab the ingredients and squeeze them together, then, when the mixture forms a rough dough, knead it gently for a minute just to bring it completely together.

3 Roll the dough into a long fat sausage, about 23cm long, then place it on the baking sheet. Bake for 25 minutes, or until light golden-brown.

4 Remove from the oven and slice into 1cm-thick pieces. A really sharp serrated knife is best, and do it gently so the biscotti sausage doesn't crumble. Put these slices back on the baking sheet and back into the oven. Immediately turn the oven down to 130°C/ Gas ½ and bake for 15 minutes.

5 Allow to cool completely and you will have a batch of beautifully baked biscotti.

PEAR, WALNUT AND MARZIPAN CRUMBLE TART
SERVES 8

1 quantity Shortcrust Pastry
(see page 20)
1kg pears, peeled, cored
and cut into 1cm dice
250g light brown
muscovado sugar
150g walnuts, chopped
1 tbsp brandy
100g marzipan

For the crumble topping
100g plain flour
75g light brown
muscovado sugar
75g salted butter

Essential equipment
23cm/9-inch loose-
bottomed flan tin

A traditional crumble is sheer bliss, and whenever my mum makes one I am completely silent as I devour it. The comforting and calming nature of the humble crumble is the inspiration for this tart.

1 Preheat the oven to 180°C/Gas 4. Make the pastry according to the instructions on page 20, then roll it out and use it to line the tin. Chill in the fridge until needed.

2 Place the diced pear in a saucepan with the sugar and set over a high heat. Stew for 10 minutes, stirring, then remove from the heat and allow to cool.

3 Once the pears have cooled, add the walnuts and brandy, and grate the marzipan in. Mix well so that everything is evenly distributed. Using a slotted spoon, pile the filling into the pastry case – you don't want too much liquid in the tart or the base of the pastry will go soggy. Bake the tart for 30 minutes. While it is baking, make the topping.

4 Mix the flour and sugar together in a mixing bowl. Cut the butter into cubes and rub this roughly into the flour, so that there are clumpy bits of crumble. Take the tart out of the oven when 30 minutes are up, sprinkle with the topping, and return to the oven for a further 20 minutes. Serve warm or cool.

AMARETTO DACQUOISE
SERVES 8

5 egg whites
285g golden caster sugar
   (to add a touch of colour)
150g ground almonds

For the filling
300ml double cream
50ml Amaretto liqueur
50g apricot jam
6 Amaretti biscuits

Essential equipment
2 baking sheets lined
   with baking paper
Piping bag with a 1cm
   plain nozzle

A dacquoise is a like sandwich cake, only made with nutty meringue layers. There is something gloriously serene about the pillowy meringue, and when it involves ground almonds, Amaretti biscuits, apricot jam and Amaretto liqueur, well, that's just the food of angels.

1 Preheat the oven to 150°C/Gas 2. On each of the lined baking sheets, draw a circle of 23cm/9-inch diameter. An easy way to do this is to draw around a 23cm cake-tin base.

2 Place the egg whites in a metal mixing bowl, or freestanding electric mixer fitted with whisk attachment, and whisk the whites until stiff. Slowly add the sugar, a tablespoon at a time, while whisking on medium speed, until all the sugar is in and is dissolved. You can check by rubbing a little of the mixture between your fingers; if it feels gritty, it needs more beating. Turn off the mixer and fold in the ground almonds.

3 Fill the piping bag with the mixture. Pipe on to the first circle in a spiral – start from the centre and spiral out until you have a large, flattish disc. Do the same with the other. Place in the warm oven, immediately turn the temperature down to 130°C/ Gas ½ and allow to dry out for 60 minutes. After 60 minutes, turn the oven off but leave the discs in there until cool, with the oven door slightly ajar. When cool, peel off the paper.

4 Place one disc on a large flat plate, upside down: in other words, with the side that was in contact with the paper facing up. Whip the cream to soft, floppy peaks and fold in the liqueur. Dollop this boozy cream on to the disc and spread out evenly. Beat the apricot jam with a spoon until loose, then drizzle over the cream. Crumble the Amaretti biscuits over the top, then finish with the second disc, the right way up.

LAVENDER AND RASPBERRY VICTORIA SPONGE

SERVES 8

80ml milk
1 tsp edible lavender flowers
225g salted butter,
    at room temperature
225g Lavender Sugar
    (see page 25)
4 eggs
250g self-raising flour

For the buttercream
160g salted butter,
    at room temperature
440g icing sugar
50ml lavender milk
    (see above)

To finish
4 tbsp raspberry jam
300g fresh raspberries

Essential equipment
2×20cm/8-inch loose-
    bottomed sandwich tins,
    bases greased and lined
Pastry brush

Sometimes it is the simplest things in life that can answer the most fundamental questions. Whenever I am feeling anxious or on edge, it is often a slice of Victoria sponge and a cup of tea that will calm my nerves. This Victoria sponge not only relaxes for its traditional comforting qualities, but also because it contains lavender sugar, to ensure complete calm. The beautiful buttercream coating is lavender-infused too.

1 Preheat the oven to 180°C/Gas 4.

2 To make the cake batter, first infuse the milk by pouring it into a small saucepan with the lavender flowers and heating over a low heat for about 10 minutes. Leave to cool completely, then strain into a bowl to remove the flowers.

3 Cream the butter and sugar together in a mixing bowl using a wooden spoon or electric beaters, or in the bowl of a freestanding electric mixer with paddle attachment if you have one, until paler in colour and lighter in texture. Then add the eggs one at a time, and beat in until you have a smooth mixture. Finally, fold in the flour and 30ml of the lavender milk.

CONTINUED OVERLEAF

4 Divide the mixture between the two prepared sandwich tins. Bake for 20–25 minutes, or until nicely golden brown and a skewer inserted into the centre of each cake comes out clean. (To ensure an even rise and colour in both cakes, bake them on the same rack, or switch them around after 15 minutes.) Remove from the oven and allow to cool slightly before removing from the tins and leaving on a wire rack until completely cold.

5 Meanwhile, make the buttercream. Beat the butter until very soft, then add the icing sugar and mix together. I find it easiest to use a food processor with blade attachment for this, because then you can blitz it and not worry about the icing sugar powder covering you and the kitchen. When the butter is well incorporated into the icing sugar, pour in the 50ml lavender milk and beat to a smooth buttercream.

6 Take one cake and place it base down on a cake stand or serving plate. Spread with 2 tablespoons of the raspberry jam, and cover with one third of the buttercream – I find it best to dollop it on and then spread it out. Then place the other cake top-down on this (I like the upper surface of the cake to be really flat). Spread the remaining buttercream on top of the cake and down the sides. Arrange the fresh raspberries on top.

7 Put the remaining raspberry jam (2 tablespoons) in a saucepan with 1 tablespoon of water, place over a medium heat and bring to the boil. Pass through a sieve, then, while the jam is still warm, use it to glaze the raspberries, painting it on with a pastry brush.

CHAPTER FOUR

THE MOOD FOR FOOD AND LOVE

I love to love. Whether it's the paternal, doting love I have for my nephews and nieces, or the passionate love I have for my partner, I am just love sick. When I was a tiny tot I went to nursery school and was constantly told off for hassling one particular child. I remember it vividly. She had fluffy white-blonde hair that stuck up like a dandelion clock. She enthralled me, so I followed her around all the time, trying to pick her up and cuddle her. It was like *Of Mice and Men*, though less brutally fatal.

Even now, I am head over heels for all my friends and family, so I bake for them as often as I can. I can't help it: I'm a love-driven feeder. Whenever there is a get-together, I am there with an array of baked goodies, chasing everyone around, forcing them to eat.

GOAT'S CHEESE AND CARAMELIZED RED ONION YEASTED FLATBREADS
MAKES 6

500g strong white flour,
  plus extra for dusting
10g salt
10g fast-action yeast
350ml tepid water
2 red onions
7 tbsp sunflower oil
1 tbsp balsamic vinegar
1 tbsp light brown
  muscovado sugar
150g hard goat's cheese
Salt and pepper
4 sprigs of thyme,
  very finely chopped

This flavour combination has been around for donkey's years, and with reason; it is a beautiful balance of sharp, tangy and sweet. These flatbreads are like bready clouds. On frying they puff up and fill with steam, which not only cooks the inside of the breads, but also keeps them deliciously soft and fluffy. For me, these have to be eaten in the company of friends or family. I love the bread dipped first in hummus and then in a sweet chilli sauce.

1 Put the flour in a mixing bowl and stir in the salt and yeast. Pour the water slowly into the flour, mixing into a rough dough with your hands or a wooden spoon.

2 Tip the dough out on to the worktop and knead for 10 minutes or until it is smooth and elastic. If you have a freestanding electric mixer, you can do this with the dough hook, which will take about 6 minutes. Ball the dough up, place it in a floured mixing bowl and cover with a damp tea towel. Leave to rise for 1 hour or until doubled in size.

3 While the dough is rising, peel the red onions and finely slice them into thin half moons. Put them in a saucepan with 1 tablespoon of the sunflower oil and place over a medium heat. Allow the onion slices to soften but not colour – about 10 minutes – then add

the vinegar and sugar and mix together. Cook slowly for a further 10 minutes, stirring occasionally, until the onions are soft and caramelized. Remove from the heat and allow to cool completely. Once cooled, crumble the goat's cheese into small nuggets of about 1cm and stir into the caramelized onions, adding a pinch of salt and pepper to season, and the finely chopped thyme.

4 Once the dough has doubled in size, tip it out on to the worktop and knock it back – in other words, knead it briefly to knock out the excess air and return the dough to the smooth elasticity you had before. Divide into 6 balls.

5 Take one ball and roll it out on a well-floured surface using a floured rolling pin until it is about 10cm in diameter. Take a sixth of the onion and cheese mixture and place it in the centre of the flatbread (see overleaf). Fold the edges of the flatbread over to cover the filling, then roll this out again, this time into a flatbread of about 18cm in diameter. Repeat with the 5 remaining portions of dough and filling. If you wish to pile the flatbreads up ready for frying, remember to flour each one very well first so they don't stick together.

6 Heat 1 tbsp of sunflower oil in a heavy frying pan over a high heat. When hot, fry one of the flatbreads for about 1 minute, or until the underside is nicely dark brown. Flip over and fry for another minute. Place on a dinner plate, with another plate inverted on top to keep it warm. Quickly but carefully wipe out the pan with a clean, damp dishcloth, return to the heat, add another tablespoon of oil, and fry the next flatbread. Do this after frying each one to avoid having a smoky kitchen. As the flatbreads are done, stack them up between the plates to keep them warm and soft. Serve as soon as they are all done.

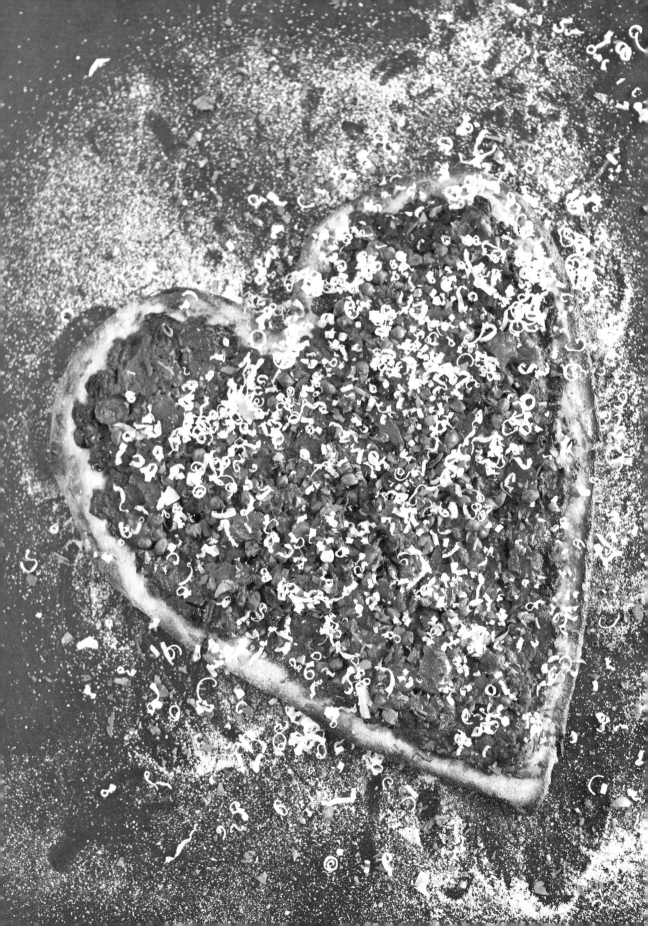

PIZZA PUTTANESCA

MAKES 1 PIZZA FOR LOVERS TO SHARE

For the dough
50g instant polenta/cornmeal
50g strong wholemeal flour
125g strong white flour
7g fast-action yeast (1 sachet)
5g salt
140ml tepid water

For the topping
1 tbsp olive oil
1 red onion, finely chopped
2 garlic cloves, crushed
  or finely chopped
400g tin chopped tomatoes
6 anchovies from a jar/tin,
  roughly chopped
80g black olives,
  roughly chopped
3 tsp capers from a jar
1 red chilli, finely chopped
Small handful finely chopped
  parsley for scattering
30g freshly grated
  Parmesan cheese

Essential equipment
Large baking sheet

Forgive me but I couldn't resist putting this 'prostitute's pizza' into my enamoured chapter. When you share it with a lover, you'll see that it isn't a sordid thing at all, but a delicious, passionate pizza that is perfect after a bit of, well, you know what ... Puttanesca was originally a pasta sauce, and one that I practically lived on when I spent a summer in Rome and Milan, working for a perfume manufacturer. The days were long and the offices were hot, but it was all worth it when I got to tuck into my favourite dish in the evenings. Thanks to the olives and anchovies, this has a bold and gutsy flavour, along with a lip-tingling spiciness from the chillies, which is never a bad thing.

1 For the dough, put the polenta and flours into a mixing bowl with the yeast and stir together, then stir in the salt. Add the water, then use a wooden spoon or your hands to bring the ingredients together into a rough dough.

CONTINUED OVERLEAF

2 Turn out on to the worktop and knead for about 10 minutes until you have a smooth and elastic dough (there will be a few grainy bits from the polenta and wholemeal flour). Alternatively, knead for about 6 minutes in an electric mixer fitted with a dough hook. Allow the dough to rise in an oiled bowl covered with a damp tea towel for 1 hour or until doubled in size.

3 When the dough has risen, place it on the large baking sheet and roll it out into a rough circle of about 28cm diameter, or make a heart shape, if you feel adventurous. Allow to rise for a second hour.

4 Meanwhile, preheat the oven to 220°C/Gas 7. Make the topping by heating the olive oil in a saucepan over a medium heat and frying the onion for about 5 minutes or until softened. Add the garlic and fry for a further minute, then add the tomatoes, anchovies, black olives, capers and chilli. Allow this to simmer for 10 minutes, or until thick and spreadable, then take off the heat and set aside to cool slightly.

5 Spread the topping over the risen pizza base, leaving a 1cm crust – there might be a few tablespoons of topping left for the cook to snack on – then slide the baking sheet into the oven and bake for 15–20 minutes or until the crust is crispy and the underneath is firm.

6 Finish with a sprinkling of parsley and a grating of Parmesan, then cut into whatever size slices you can manage, and eat in bed with your hands.

FRANGELICO FONDANTS
MAKES 4

100g milk chocolate,
  roughly chopped
100g salted butter, cubed
100g dark brown
  muscovado sugar
1 tbsp golden syrup
50ml double cream
50g self-raising flour
2 eggs
5 tbsp Frangelico liqueur

Essential equipment
4×180ml/6fl oz pudding
  moulds, greased and floured
Deep baking tray

This is the ultimate sin: a boozy hazelnut and chocolate pudding with a molten filling that just oozes out. If, unlike me, you are strong enough to share these with someone, they make a perfect sexy supper. What's more, with two of you and four of these, there will definitely be a round two ...

1 Preheat the oven to 180°C/Gas 4. Place the pudding moulds in the freezer. Have boiling water at the ready for the bain marie.

2 Put the chocolate into a medium saucepan with the butter, sugar and golden syrup and place over a medium heat. Stir until the chocolate and butter have melted together and the sugar has dissolved. Remove from the heat and whisk in the cream, flour, eggs and Frangelico until you have a smooth, velvety batter. Divide this equally between the 4 prepared moulds.

3 Put the moulds in the deep baking tray and place in the oven. Fill the baking tray with boiling water until it comes halfway up the sides of the moulds, making a bain marie. Bake for 25 minutes, then remove from the oven and take the moulds out of the water at once to stop them cooking further. Turn them out on to plates and start the fondant fun.

CHOCOLATE, HAZELNUT AND SOUR CHERRY CELEBRATION PLAITED WREATH

SERVES AT LEAST 10

For the bread
500g strong white flour,
  plus extra for dusting
5g salt
40g caster sugar
10g fast-action yeast
40g butter, melted and cooled
150ml tepid water
150ml tepid milk
1 egg

For the filling
6 tbsp chocolate hazelnut
  spread, such as Nutella
125g chopped hazelnuts
200g dried sour cherries,
  or cranberries

Essential equipment
Baking sheet lined
  with baking paper

This is a family feeding loaf. Not only does this look great, but it tastes incredible, and you can guarantee there will be nothing left when served at a family feast. This filling is my absolute favourite, but you could use whatever you fancied. Mincemeat is perfect at Christmas.

1 Put the flour in a mixing bowl and stir the salt in, then add the sugar and the yeast. Put the butter into a jug with the water, milk and egg, beat together, and pour into the dry ingredients.

2 With your hands or a wooden spoon, mix everything together into a rough dough, then tip out on to the worktop and knead for about 10 minutes, or until smooth and elastic. (Or use a mixer with a dough hook for about 6 minutes.) Place in an oiled bowl, cover with cling film or a damp cloth, and allow the dough to rise for 1 hour or until doubled in size.

CONTINUED OVERLEAF

CHOCOLATE, HAZELNUT AND SOUR CHERRY CELEBRATION PLAITED WREATH CONTINUED

3 Once the dough has doubled in size, flour the worktop and tip the dough out on to it. With a floured rolling pin, roll the dough out into a rectangle of about 30×35cm – remember to keep moving the dough about and reflouring underneath it to prevent it sticking to the worktop.

4 Prepare the filling. Warm the spread in a small saucepan over a medium heat until it is runny, then spread it on to the surface of the dough, covering it completely. Sprinkle over the hazelnuts and cherries or cranberries.

5 Working from the longer side of the dough, roll it up tightly into a big sausage. Turn the sausage so that it is vertical, then, with a sharp knife, cut it in half along its length, so you have two long half sausages. Position them so that the cut, layered edges face upwards, then pinch together the two ends furthest away from you. Wrap the dough half-sausages round one another, ensuring you keep the cut edges upwards, until they are braided together. Pinch the near ends together, then bring the two ends of the fat braid together into a wreath, and squash them together. Place on the baking sheet.

6 Allow the dough wreath to rise for 45 minutes. Preheat the oven to 180°C/Gas 4.

7 Bake the risen wreath for 25–35 minutes, or until the dough is golden brown and the chocolate spread has melted slightly. If the wreath starts to brown too much during baking, cover it with a sheet of foil. Remove from the oven and allow to cool on a cooling wrack until completely cold.

BACI DI DAMA

MAKES ABOUT 50

For the gianduja filling
   (if making)
150g skinless hazelnuts
225g milk chocolate
60g caster sugar
½ tsp salt
60g sunflower oil

For the baci di dama
200g skinless hazelnuts
   or ground hazelnuts
200g caster sugar
1 egg white
170g salted butter
210g plain flour
40g cornflour

Essential equipment
2 baking sheets lined
   with baking paper

These bite-sized Italian treats ('ladies' kisses') are so good that you can guarantee every one will be greedily gobbled up. Who could resist chocolate hazelnut spread sandwiched between hazelnut biscuits? If you are using whole hazelnuts, you really do need to make the biscuits and the filling in a food processor. If you don't have one, you can always buy ground hazelnuts instead. This recipe also calls for making your own gianduja, which is a chocolate hazelnut spread like Nutella. If you wanted you could use Nutella instead.

1 If you are making the filling, place the hazelnuts in the food processor with the chocolate, sugar and salt. Blitz together into crumbs. Place the oil in a small saucepan over a high heat and warm until you can only just hold your finger in. Turn the processor back on and slowly pour in the warm oil. Process into a paste before decanting into a bowl. Cover with cling film and refrigerate until needed.

2 To make the biscuits, place the hazelnuts and sugar in a food processor and blitz. Add the egg white and butter and blitz again to a paste before adding the flours and pulsing into a dough. Remove the dough from the processor and knead by hand for a minute or two until smooth. Chill the mixture for at least 30 minutes. Preheat the oven to 200°C/Gas 6.

3 Weigh out balls of dough of around 7g each, and place these on the lined baking sheets. You will have about 100 dough balls.

4 Bake the baci di dama for 12–15 minutes, or until slightly cracked and a very pale golden brown on top, with the bases slightly darker. Allow to cool before sandwiching in pairs with gianduja or Nutella.

GOLDEN HEART CAKE

SERVES 8–12

For the caramel and fruit
200g white caster sugar
2 tbsp water
3 apples (baking or eating),
   peeled and thinly sliced
Handful of dried cranberries
Zest of 1 orange: one-third
   (use the rest for the sponge)

For the sponge
170g salted butter,
   at room temperature
170g golden caster sugar
170g self-raising flour, sifted
3 eggs, also at room
   temperature
50ml milk
Seeds from 1 vanilla pod, or
   1 tsp vanilla paste or extract
Zest of 1 orange: two-thirds
½ tsp bicarbonate of soda
1 tsp lemon juice

For the spun-sugar top
200g white caster sugar
2 tbsp water

Essential equipment
23cm/9-inch springform
   heart-shaped cake tin,
   greased

This is the ultimate cake to serve to the whole family after Sunday lunch. I first made this when I was at my mum and stepdad's house for a weekend, using the apples from their garden.

1 To make the caramel, stir the sugar and water together in a saucepan, then place over a high heat and allow the sugar to melt without stirring it again. Let it bubble ferociously, and when it turns a deep amber and the bubbles start to reduce in size, remove from the heat and pour into the bottom of the cake tin. Dot with apples and cranberries, and scatter with zest.

2 For the sponge, cream together the butter and sugar. (Easiest with an electric whisk or in a freestanding mixer.) Add one tablespoon of the sifted flour and one egg. Mix well, then add more flour with another egg. Repeat this until all eggs and then all the flour have gone in. Add the milk, vanilla and orange zest. In a cup, mix together the bicarbonate of soda and lemon juice, and fold this into the batter.

3 Pour the batter over the apples and cranberries and bang the tin on the worktop once or twice to ensure there are no trapped air bubbles. Slide into the oven and bake for 40–50 minutes, or until a skewer inserted into the centre comes out clean.

4 When the cake is ready, leave in the tin for 3 minutes to cool, then turn out on to a cooling rack and leave until completely cold. Clean the base of the heart-shaped tin, dry it and grease it well. Repeat the caramel-making process from step 1, then pour it over the base of the cake tin in lines to make a caramel mesh. Allow to cool. When completely cold, gently place the spun-sugar heart on top of the cake.

BUNCH OF ROSES MADELEINES
MAKES 16

100g salted butter
100g caster sugar
2 eggs
100g plain flour, sifted
A few drops of rosewater

For the fondant icing (optional)
200g ready-to-roll fondant icing
40ml water
A few drops of rosewater
Pink or red food colouring
100g white chocolate

Essential equipment
16-hole madeleine tin,
  greased and floured
Freestanding or hand-held
  electric mixer
Piping bag with a number
  2 nozzle

Baking for someone is a far better 'I love you' than giving them a bunch of flowers from the local petrol station. If, however, you're a sucker for tradition, then why not make this hybrid: rose-flavoured madeleines. They are beautiful rolled in sugar, but I prefer them covered in a pink rose-scented fondant, then drizzled with white chocolate.

1 Preheat the oven to 190°C/Gas 5. Place the madeleine tin in the freezer.

2 Put the butter in a saucepan and heat on high until melted and just starting to brown. Set aside.

3 Place the sugar and eggs in a freestanding mixer and whisk on full speed for about 4 minutes, or until frothy, light and the mixture falls in ribbons from the whisk. You can also do this in a bowl with a hand-held electric mixer, but it may take a few minutes longer.

4 Add the sifted flour by pouring it down the side of the bowl. This is better than sifting straight into the eggs, which could deflate the mix. Pour the butter down the side of the bowl in the same way, then fold in the flour and butter until you have a smooth, light batter. Add rosewater to taste.

5 Remove the madeleine tin from the freezer. Spoon about 2 teaspoons of batter into each hole. Bake for 9–10 minutes, or until the edges are just beginning to brown. Remove immediately from the tins and place on a cooling rack, ridged side up, and allow to cool.

6 Beat the fondant icing until it breaks apart, then add the water and whisk into a thick, pourable icing. Add rosewater to taste, and the colouring to make it a soft pink, then spoon it over the madeleines.

7 Melt the white chocolate in a bowl set over a pan of barely simmering water, then spoon into the piping bag and quickly and confidently pipe the white chocolate over the madeleines. Allow the chocolate to set before sharing the madeleines with one you love.

PASSIONFRUIT TART
SERVES 8

1 quantity Rich Sweet
   Shortcrust Pastry
   (see page 21)
11 passionfruit
120ml double cream
140g caster sugar
5 eggs, beaten

Essential equipment
23cm/9-inch loose-
   bottomed flan tin
Food processor

I adore passionfruit, so much so that I can quite easily eat the pulp of three passionfruit with a spoon and a smile. Sometimes, though, I try to be a little more refined, and this tart is perfect for those occasions.

1 Line the flan tin with the pastry and blind-bake (see page 19).

2 Preheat the oven to 170°C/Gas 3.

3 Scrape the pulp of 9 of the passionfruit into a food processor and blitz for a few seconds to loosen everything up. Sieve the juice into a jug, ensuring you get every last drop, then discard the seeds and remaining pulp. Stir the cream, sugar and eggs into the passionfruit juice.

4 Put the blind-baked pastry case back in the oven, then pull out its shelf and pour in the passionfruit filling. Bake for 30–35 minutes, or until the filling is just about set, but wobbles slightly in the middle when the tart is moved.

5 Allow to cool completely before removing from the tin and putting on a serving plate. Scatter with the seeds of the remaining passionfruit before serving.

ROSE AND LYCHEE MERINGUE HEARTS

MAKES 10

5 egg whites
285g caster sugar

For the topping
40g unsalted butter
110g icing sugar
40g lychees from a can,
    finely chopped
30 raspberries
10 rose petals
Caster sugar, for dipping

Essential equipment
2 baking sheets lined
    with baking paper
9cm/3½-inch heart-shaped
    cookie cutter
Piping bag with a large
    star nozzle

Irresistible in both form and flavour, these are perfect for sharing with the whole family. As the flavours are light, this makes a great dessert after a heavy meal.

1 Preheat the oven to 140°C/Gas 1. On the paper you've lined the baking sheets with, draw around the heart-shaped cookie cutter 10 times – 5 per sheet.

2 Put the egg whites in a large, ideally metal mixing bowl and whisk until they form stiff peaks. This is best done with a hand-held electric mixer or in a freestanding mixer with whisk attachment. Continue whisking on a medium speed and add the sugar a tablespoon at a time, whisking for 5 seconds or so after each addition and resisting the temptation to hurry. Once the sugar is well incorporated, your meringue should be stiff and very glossy.

3 Fill the piping bag with the meringue and pipe it on to the heart templates – I start around the edges and then work my way in, in a heart-shaped spiral. When you have piped all 10 hearts, place in the preheated oven and immediately reduce the temperature to 130°C/Gas ½. Bake for 45–60 minutes, then turn the oven off but leave the heartlets in for an hour to cool, with the oven door slightly ajar.

4 While the meringues cool, make the topping by beating the butter with a wooden spoon until soft and pliable. Gently stir in the icing sugar and mix into a smooth buttercream. If you have a food processor, throw the butter and icing sugar into that and blitz. Fold the lychees into the buttercream.

5 Put buttercream on each meringue, then embellish with 3 raspberries and a rose petal dipped in sugar.

WHITE CHOCOLATE AND LEMON TARTLETS

MAKES 12

1 quantity Rich Sweet
    Shortcrust Pastry
    (see page 21)
200g white chocolate,
    finely chopped
50ml cream
Zest of 1 small lemon
2 tbsp Limoncello liqueur

Essential equipment
12-hole shallow bun tray
7.5cm/3-inch cookie cutter
Baking paper and beans/rice

I had already made the Chocolate Orange Tartlets (see page 202) when I thought I really should do a version with white chocolate. These tartlets are such a romantic thing. Something about the purity of the white chocolate, and the sharp hit of the lemon and Limoncello, make them the perfect end to a romantic supper.

1 Make the pastry according to the recipe on page 21, then chill in the fridge for 30 minutes. Preheat the oven to 180°C/Gas 4.

2 Roll out the chilled pastry to about 4mm thick, and cut out 12 circles using the cookie cutter. Line the bun tray with these pastry circles, pricking the base of each one with a fork. Cut out 12 squares of baking paper, larger than the holes of the tin, and line the pastry with them. Fill each square with ceramic baking beans, or dried rice, and place in the oven. Bake for 12 minutes, then remove from the oven, remove the paper and beans, and return to the oven to bake for a further 5 minutes. Allow the pastry cases to cool completely.

3 Make the filling by placing the chocolate in a heatproof bowl. Heat the cream in a small saucepan over a medium heat, until it is just hot enough that you can't hold your finger in there. Stir in most of the lemon zest – keep some choice strands for decoration – and the Limoncello, then pour over the chocolate. Stir together until the chocolate has melted and you have a glossy ganache. If the chocolate doesn't melt completely, rinse the saucepan, fill it with hot water from the tap and place back on a medium heat. Set the bowl over the saucepan and stir constantly until the chocolate is thick and glossy.

4 Fill each cooled pastry shell to the brim with white chocolate ganache, then top each tart with a little lemon zest.

CHAPTER FIVE
EDIBLE NIRVANA

I wanted to include a chapter of recipes
I had created when everything was calm
both in my life and in my mind. Needless
to say, I struggled. There always seems to be
something niggling away at me. So I turned
to my mum and asked her for a little help in
finding my elusive tranquillity. She replied,
'John, love, you've never been tranquil.
When you were a little boy, the health visitor
suggested I give you sedatives.'

So that says it all: I am never actually tranquil.
Some people dream of relaxing on a sandy
beach under a draping palm tree, but the
thought of that bores me to tears. On reflection,
though, I do find a form of serenity through
certain things I bake – in the exotic taste of
coconut or in other fragrant ingredients.
The recipes in this chapter, then, are for the
moments when you need some tranquillity
in your life, some edible nirvana.

COCONUT AND LEMON BAKEWELL

SERVES 8-12

1 quantity Shortcrust Pastry
   (see page 20)
1 egg white, beaten

*For the coconut
frangipane filling*
175g unsalted butter,
   at room temperature
175g caster sugar
4 eggs
85g desiccated coconut
90g ground almonds
1 tbsp flour
Zest of 2 lemons

For the lemon curd filling
150g home-made Lemon
   Curd (see page 26) or
   best quality shop-bought
1 egg yolk

For the icing
250g icing sugar
2 tbsp water
1 tbsp desiccated coconut
Zest of half a lemon

Essential equipment
25cm/10-inch loose-
   bottomed fluted tart tin
Baking paper or foil and beans
   or rice for blind-baking
Piping bag with 3cm plain
   nozzle (or cut the end off
   a disposable bag)

I adore coconut and lemon. There is something about the sharp tang cutting through the milky sweetness that just dances on the tastebuds. This is a Bakewell tart but with coconut frangipane and lemon curd instead of the usual sponge and raspberry jam.

1 Make the pastry according to the instructions on page 20, then roll out and use to line the tart tin, pressing the pastry into the grooves. Prick the base with a fork and place in the freezer for 30 minutes.

2 Preheat the oven to 190°C/Gas 5.

3 For the frangipane, beat the sugar and butter very well until light and fluffy. Add the eggs and mix well. Gently fold in the coconut, almonds, flour and zest, then set aside.

4 Beat the lemon curd with the egg yolk and set aside.

5 Line the pastry case with baking paper or foil and fill with beans or rice. Bake for 15 minutes, then remove the beans and paper and bake for another 12 minutes. Remove from the oven, paint the base and sides with the egg white and return to the oven for one more minute – this will create a waterproof coat on the pastry to prevent any soggy bottoms.

6 Allow the pastry to cool slightly before spreading the curd over the base. Fill a piping bag with the frangipane and pipe it on to the lemon curd in concentric rings, until the lemon curd can no longer be seen. Return to the oven for 30–35 minutes, or until the frangipane is a golden brown and very slightly wobbly. Remove and allow to cool.

7 Put the icing sugar in a bowl. Slowly add the water, mixing until you have a pourable but thick icing. When the tart has cooled, pour the icing on top, and sprinkle with desiccated coconut and lemon zest.

ITALIAN FEEDING FRENZY FOCACCIA
SERVES 8–10

600g strong white flour
2 tsp dried oregano
1 large sprig rosemary,
    finely chopped
10g salt
10g fast-action yeast
80g black pitted olives,
    roughly chopped
80g sun-dried tomatoes
    from a jar, roughly chopped
30ml olive oil, plus extra
    for drizzling
480ml tepid water

To serve
Good quality extra
    virgin olive oil
Sea salt flakes

Essential equipment
Deep-sided baking tray,
    at least 23×30cm/9×12
    inches, oiled (use the
    oil from the sun-dried
    tomato jar)

My family loves a good feast, so on a summery Sunday afternoon we will often be in the garden, circling a table of fabulous foods. This is a bread I always add to the mix, because a feast wouldn't be a feast without my focaccia.

1 Place the flour in a large mixing bowl and stir in the oregano, rosemary and salt, followed by the yeast, olives and sun-dried tomatoes. Mix the olive oil with the water and slowly add to the flour, stirring vigorously with a wooden spoon. This will be a very wet dough. Now oil your hands and manipulate the dough in the bowl, stretching and kneading it as much as possible for about 10 minutes. Cover the bowl with a damp tea towel and leave for 1–1½ hours or until the dough has almost tripled in volume.

2 Gently remove the risen dough and place it in the oiled baking tray. Stretch it so it roughly fits. You don't need to knock this back, as the larger bubbles will give a great texture to the dough. Leave to rise for a further hour. Preheat the oven to 230°C/Gas 8.

3 Dip your finger in flour and make indentations in the risen focaccia, in even lines. Make sure you press right down to the bottom to create the characteristic dimples. Drizzle with oil and bake for 30 minutes.

4 Remove and drizzle with even more oil, this time some good quality extra virgin, and sprinkle with plenty of sea salt flakes. Serve at once.

APRICOT AND PECAN HERB LOAF

SERVES 8–10

500g strong white flour
10g salt
10g fast-action yeast
1 tsp dried thyme
1 tsp dried oregano
1 tbsp olive oil
350ml tepid water
150g pecans, roughly chopped
125g dried apricots,
   roughly chopped

Essential equipment
2lb (900g) loaf tin, oiled with
   olive oil and dusted with flour
Baking sheet
Spray bottle filled with water

Kneading bread dough is a sure-fire anger-management method. I also find it soothing. If you are already in a calm, relaxed mood, then the process of kneading will enhance that euphoric state. The flavours of this loaf are mouth-watering and it is perfect slathered in butter.

1 Place the flour and salt in a mixing bowl. Add the yeast and herbs, and mix. Add the oil to the water, then slowly add to the dry ingredients, mixing with a wooden spoon as you do so. Turn the contents of the bowl out on to the worktop and knead for 8 minutes, then add the nuts and fruit and knead for a further 2 minutes, or until the dough is smooth and elastic. Place the dough in an oiled bowl, cover with cling film and allow to rise for 1 hour, or until doubled in size. If making this in a freestanding mixer with dough hook, knead the dough for 4 minutes before adding the nuts and fruit and kneading for a further 2 minutes.

2 When the dough has risen, remove from the bowl, knock back to get rid of excess air, then roll into a fat sausage the length of the loaf tin. Put the dough sausage in the tin, placing the folded side underneath and the neat, rounded side on top, then cover and allow to rise for a further 45 minutes.

3 Preheat the oven to 230°C/Gas 8, with a baking sheet on the shelf you will bake your bread on.

4 Put the dough in its tin on to the baking sheet in the hot oven. Spray a mist of water into the oven before quickly shutting the door. Bake for 30 minutes, or until beautifully golden, and the loaf sounds hollow when tipped from the tin and tapped on the bottom. Allow to cool before devouring.

LEMON MERINGUE CAKE
SERVES 8

For the cakes
225g salted butter,
  at room temperature
225g caster sugar
4 eggs
Zest of 2 lemons
225g self-raising flour
75g ground almonds
Juice of 1 lemon

For the lemon drizzle
Juice of 1 lemon
75g caster sugar

For the Italian meringue
4 egg whites
225g caster sugar
3 tbsp water

For the filling
4 tbsp home-made Lemon
  Curd (see page 26) or
  best quality shop-bought

Essential equipment
2×20cm/8-inch loose-bottomed
  sandwich tins, greased and
  lined with baking paper
Sugar thermometer
Piping bag with a large
  star nozzle
Cook's blowtorch (optional)

Lemon meringue is a timeless classic. It has been done thousands of times and I personally don't think I will ever get bored with it. What I wanted to do here was to change it ever so slightly, not just to make it my own, but to demonstrate how easy it is to use a classic flavour combination in another way. This cake version consists of two layers of a lemon drizzle cake sandwiching Italian meringue and lemon curd, then covered in more blistered and burnished Italian meringue. Italian meringue has got a reputation for being difficult to make, but if you follow the steps carefully, you won't have a problem.

1 Preheat the oven to 160°C/Gas 3.

2 Start by making the cakes. Cream the butter and sugar together in a bowl until much paler in colour and lighter in texture. You could do this with a wooden spoon, but it will be quicker and easier with an electric whisk or in a freestanding electric mixer with paddle attachment. Add the eggs, one at a time, and mix until well incorporated, adding the lemon zest with the last egg. If the mixture starts to look a little curdled, add a tablespoon of the flour.

3 Sift the flour on to the eggy mixture, then add the ground almonds and lemon juice, and fold in gently. Divide the mixture between the 2 prepared tins.

4 Bake for 25–30 minutes, until a skewer inserted into the centre of the cakes comes out clean, or the cakes have stopped 'singing'. By this I mean that they have stopped making a gentle crackly bubbling sound. If both cakes don't fit on a single shelf, switch them around halfway through to ensure they bake evenly.

CONTINUED OVERLEAF

LEMON MERINGUE CAKE CONTINUED

5 While the cakes are baking, make the drizzle. Place the lemon juice and sugar in a small saucepan and set over a high heat. Bring to the boil then reduce the heat and allow the syrup to simmer for a minute or two. Remove from the heat and set to one side.

6 Remove the cakes from the oven. Allow to cool for a few minutes in their tins, then release them and leave on a cooling rack to cool completely.

7 Make the Italian meringue. Place the egg whites in a heatproof mixing bowl – preferably metal – and whisk using a hand-held electric mixer. You could also do this in a freestanding electric mixer with whisk attachment. Beat the egg whites until they are at soft peaks: when you lift the whisk out of them they just hold a peak, albeit a floppy one.

8 Place the sugar and water in a medium saucepan over a medium-high heat, and clip the sugar thermometer in place. If your thermometer doesn't have a clip, simply hold it. Do not stir the mixture at any point, just leave it to boil and bubble away. When the thermometer reads 118°C or 'softball stage' – after about 5 minutes – remove the pan from the heat immediately, being careful not to burn yourself.

9 Turn the mixer for the egg whites back on to medium speed and gently pour the sugar syrup down the side of the bowl. Continue whisking on medium until the meringue has cooled to room temperature. This will take about 6 or 7 minutes.

10 Place one cake, bottom down, on a cake stand. Spoon half the drizzle over and allow to soak in for a minute. Spread with the lemon curd. Fill the piping bag with meringue and pipe one third of it on top. Take the other cake and place it upside down on top of the meringue, so you have a flat top to the cake. Spoon the remaining drizzle on top. Pipe the rest of the meringue in spikes all over the cake, and finally, for a professional and dramatic finish, burnish with the cook's blowtorch.

EASTERN SWEET SPRING ROLLS
SERVES 6

100g dried figs,
  roughly chopped
150g dried prunes,
  roughly chopped
100g mini marshmallows
50g desiccated coconut
1 tbsp honey
½ tsp mixed spice
½ tsp rosewater
75g pistachio kernels,
  roughly bashed into shards
6 sheets of filo pastry

Essential equipment
Food processor
Deep-fat fryer or large
  saucepan filled with
  2 litres sunflower oil

Now these truly are edible nirvana. As you bite into one, the crisp filo pastry breaks away between your teeth, which then slowly sink into a marshmallowy, fruity centre full of the flavours of gentle spice, honey and pistachio. I love these served with a big dollop of Greek yoghurt, a drizzle of honey and a scattering of pistachios. They are best eaten straightaway, although they are also perfectly delicious when cooled.

1 Place the figs, prunes, marshmallows, coconut, honey, spice and rosewater in a food processor and blitz into a gritty mush. Add the pistachio kernels and pulse a few times until well distributed – you don't want to lose the texture of the nuts.

2 Take a sheet of filo pastry and fold it in half across the length. (Keep the other filo in its packet or under a barely damp tea towel so it doesn't dry out.) Roll a sixth of the fruity mush into a fat sausage, shorter than the width of the filo pastry, and place at one end of the pastry. Tuck the sides of pastry over the filling, then roll the pastry and filling up into a spring roll. Repeat with the remaining filling and sheets of filo.

3 Heat the oil to 180°C, either using the thermostat on the fryer or by placing a sugar thermometer into the pan of oil. Fry 2 or 3 rolls at a time, for 4 minutes each – they should go a deep golden brown. Remove with a slotted spoon and drain on a piece of kitchen paper.

PEAR AND GINGER TARTE FINE
SERVES 8–10

320g (approx.) roll of all-butter
   puff pastry, thawed if frozen
3–4 large Conference pears,
   topped and tailed
50g light brown
   muscovado sugar
1 tsp ground ginger
30g unsalted butter,
   very cold and chopped
   into tiny squares
1 egg, beaten with a tiny
   pinch of salt, for glazing
Icing sugar, to serve

Essential equipment
Baking sheet

This is a delicious, fruity indulgence and really easy to make, especially if you use shop-bought, ready-rolled puff pastry (no pastry snob here). Pear and ginger are a classic twosome.

1 Preheat the oven to 200°C/Gas 6.

2 Unroll the pastry on to the baking sheet and, with a sharp knife, score a large rectangle 1cm in from the edges. Put into the fridge until needed.

3 Peel the pears if you want to. (I don't bother.) Halve them lengthways, then, with a very sharp knife, cut slices, again lengthways, around 2mm thick. I don't bother to core the pears, either – not only are their cores fairly soft anyway, they will soften as they cook. Place in a mixing bowl with the sugar and ginger, and mix to coat well – I use my hands for this.

4 Remove the pastry from the fridge and arrange the pears across it – remembering to leave the 1cm margin all the way around. Scatter the finely chopped butter all over. I also like to drizzle over any juice that might be waiting in the mixing bowl.

5 Glaze the 1cm margin with the beaten egg. Pop the tarte into the oven, still on its baking sheet, and bake for 25–30 minutes, or until the edges are perfectly puffed and the pears are burnished. Allow to cool before sifting over a shower of icing sugar.

PLUM AND PINE NUT LOAF CAKE
SERVES 8–10

170g salted butter,
  at room temperature
170g light brown
  muscovado sugar
3 eggs
170g plain flour
Zest of 1 large orange
1 tbsp golden syrup
280g dried prunes,
  roughly chopped
85g pine nuts

Essential equipment
2lb (900g) loaf tin, greased
  and lined with baking paper

OK, so I've lied a little bit here – this is actually a prune and pine nut cake – but I like my title a lot more. Besides, prunes are a type of dried plum, so I'm not being completely mendacious. This should be treated like a fruit cake: baked at a low temperature for a longer time so the sugars in the fruit don't char and burn. This is gorgeous on the day it is made, and even better a day or two later. Serve in thick slices with a good cup of tea.

1 Preheat the oven to 150°C/Gas 2.

2 Put the butter and sugar into a mixing bowl, or the bowl of a freestanding electric mixer with paddle attachment, and cream together until paler in colour and lighter in texture. Add the eggs, 1 tablespoon of the flour, the orange zest and golden syrup, and beat in well until smooth. Tip in the rest of the flour – no need to sift – and beat that in too. Finally, fold in the prunes and pine nuts.

3 Dollop the mixture into the lined loaf tin and level the top with a spoon. Bake for 60–65 minutes, or until a skewer inserted into the centre comes out greasy but clean, or until the cake has stopped making a gentle crackling, bubbly sound. Allow to cool briefly in the tin, then turn out to cool completely on a rack.

SPICED APPLE AND CRANBERRY MUFFINS
MAKES 12

225g plain flour
2 tsp mixed spice
150g light brown
   muscovado sugar
2 tsp baking powder
75g dried sweetened
   cranberries
100g dried apple,
   cut into 5mm pieces
225ml milk
2 eggs
115g salted butter, melted
Seeds from 1 vanilla pod,
   or 1 tsp vanilla paste
   or extract

Essential equipment
12-hole muffin tray,
   lined with paper cases

I couldn't decide whether or not I wanted to include muffins – these and my Bakewell Muffins on page 155 – in my book because sometimes it seems that the muffin is an exhausted old cake now. But after I had browsed through my recipe notepad and made both muffins again, I knew I had to include them, because they really are so tasty. These apple and cranberry muffins bring sheer tranquillity. The spicy yet sweet taste seems to calm you instantaneously.

1 Preheat the oven to 180°C/Gas 4.

2 Put the flour, mixed spice, sugar and baking powder in a mixing bowl and rub together with your hands so that the muscovado sugar – which naturally forms little clumps – is broken up and evenly dispersed. Add the cranberries and apple.

3 In a jug, whisk together the milk, eggs, melted butter and vanilla, then slowly pour this into the bowl containing the dry ingredients. Fold together, but don't over-mix; the odd little lump of dry flour really doesn't matter. You don't want to beat the mixture because that can result in tough and chewy muffins.

4 Divide the batter between the 12 muffin cases. Gently tap the tray down on the worktop three or four times to expel any trapped air bubbles, then bake for 25–30 minutes, or until the muffins are well risen and golden brown. Allow to cool, then enjoy.

FIG AND ROSE SAVARIN
SERVES 8

225g plain flour
½ tsp salt
40g caster sugar
7g fast-action yeast (1 sachet)
4 eggs
2 tbsp milk
110g unsalted butter,
   at room temperature
125g dried figs,
   coarsely chopped

For the syrup
250g sugar
100ml water
1–3 tsp rosewater
1–2 tbsp gin

To finish
400ml double cream
2 tbsp icing sugar
Seeds from 1 vanilla pod
6–8 fresh figs, halved
   lengthways
Icing sugar to dust (optional)

Essential equipment
20cm/8-inch savarin mould,
   butter for greasing and
   caster sugar for dusting
Deep-sided baking tray
Piping bag

This is a beautiful, butter-enriched cake–bread hybrid. The soft sponge soaks up the rosewater syrup, which perfectly and exotically complements the figs.

1 To make the savarin batter, place the flour in a mixing bowl, stir in the salt and sugar, then stir the yeast through. Beat the eggs and milk in a jug and pour this into the dry ingredients. Using a wooden spoon or hand-held electric mixer, beat for about 5 minutes. (You could do this in a freestanding electric mixer with paddle attachment.) Add the butter in thirds, beating well to incorporate each addition. Finally, stir in the chopped figs. Cover the bowl with a cloth and leave the dough to prove for 1 hour.

2 Meanwhile, grease the savarin mould with butter and place it into the freezer for 10 minutes. Then grease it again and freeze until needed.

3 When the batter has rested for 1 hour, remove the savarin mould from the freezer and dust the inside with a generous amount of caster sugar, ensuring even coverage. Spoon the batter into the mould and even it out. Cover with oiled cling film and leave to rest for another hour, or until the batter has risen and is just below the rim of the mould.

4 Preheat the oven to 180°C/Gas 4.

5 Bake the batter for 20–25 minutes, or until the savarin has risen up out of the tin (though it shouldn't have muffin-topped over) and is golden brown.

CONTINUED OVERLEAF

FIG AND ROSE SAVARIN CONTINUED

6 While the savarin is baking, make the syrup by heating the sugar and water in a saucepan over a high heat. Boil for about 4 minutes, or until thick and syrupy, then remove from the heat and allow to cool. Stir in the rosewater and gin to taste.

7 Remove the savarin from the mould. Pour about a third of the scented syrup into the mould and gently place the savarin back in so it can start to soak it up. Pour the remaining syrup into a deep-sided baking tray, then invert the savarin, in its mould, into this, and leave to soak for about 5 minutes.

8 Make a crème Chantilly by whisking together the cream, icing sugar and vanilla seeds until the cream just holds its shape. Remove the soaked savarin from the mould and place on a cake stand. Pipe the crème Chantilly into the centre, then arrange the fresh figs on top. Dust with icing sugar, if you like.

WHITE CHOCOLATE AND RASPBERRY MELTING CAKE

SERVES 8

200g unsalted butter, at room
temperature, cut into cubes
100g white chocolate,
broken into pieces
4 eggs
200g caster sugar
200g self-raising flour
175g fresh raspberries
Icing sugar for dusting

For the ganache filling
200g white chocolate,
broken into pieces
250ml double cream

Essential equipment
2×20cm/8-inch round
loose-bottomed cake tins,
greased and base-lined

After a stressful day, I just want to get home as quickly as possible and get started in my kitchen. This recipe is a perfect stress-buster: not only is the method of melting butter and chocolate together somehow pacifying, but the sharp tang of the raspberries against the nostalgic sweetness of the white chocolate seems to instil serenity. I first wrote this recipe for the BBC's Good Food magazine, and the feedback from readers was brilliant.

1 Preheat the oven to 180°C/Gas 4.

2 Put the butter and chocolate in a large heatproof mixing bowl above a pan of barely simmering water, and allow them to melt and meld together slowly, stirring occasionally. Remove from the heat and set aside to cool for a minute or so.

3 When the melted butter and chocolate have cooled, add the eggs and sugar and beat with an electric mixer until you have a smooth and a consistent batter – this takes a minute or two. Sift the flour over the bowl and fold that in, along with the fresh raspberries.

CONTINUED OVERLEAF

4 Gently pour into the prepared cake tins, dividing equally between them.

5 Bake for 20–25 minutes, or until golden brown and a skewer inserted into the centre comes out clean – remember the raspberries may leave a residue on the knife; don't be fooled by their juiciness. Switch the tins halfway through baking, if you are not baking them on the same shelf. Allow to cool completely.

6 To make the ganache, put the chocolate into a heatproof bowl with 100ml of the cream. Set over a pan of barely simmering water and stir until the chocolate has melted into the cream and you are left with a smooth, glossy ganache. Leave to cool to room temperature, then beat in the rest of the cream. It takes a while for the ganache to cool and thicken, so do be patient, and don't do as I do and eat the whole thing before it's cooled.

7 When the cakes have cooled, sandwich them together – the lower one base-side down, the upper one inverted, so that you have a smooth top and bottom – with the white chocolate ganache. Dust with icing sugar just before serving.

TROPICAL SPONGE PUDDING
SERVES 8–12

Pulp of 6 large passionfruit
180g diced mango flesh
100ml milk
300g light brown
　muscovado sugar
2 eggs
60g salted butter
300g plain flour
100g desiccated coconut
Seeds from 1 vanilla pod, or
　1 tsp vanilla paste or extract
1 tsp bicarbonate of soda

For the sauce
150ml double cream
200g Passionfruit Curd
　(see page 26) or best
　quality shop-bought

Essential equipment
Food processor
35×22cm/14×9-inch
　pudding dish, greased

This has to be the lightest, fruitiest pudding out there. It's not a sweet and acidic fruit pudding, but a sponge pudding with a rounded, tender crumb, and fruit flavours that are aromatic and palate-cleansing. I love this served hot out of the oven with its cold sharp sauce.

1 Preheat the oven to 180°C/Gas 4.

2 Put the passionfruit pulp in a food processor and blitz until the pulp is juiced and free from the seeds. Strain this mixture into a bowl, making sure you get every last seed out of the processor. Discard the passionfruit seeds, then return the strained pulp to the food processor bowl along with the mango. Blitz the passionfruit and mango together.

3 Add the milk, sugar and eggs, and blitz into a sweet, fruity syrup. Add the remaining ingredients and process to a smooth batter.

4 Pour into the greased pudding dish and bake for 35–40 minutes, or until golden brown and spongy.

5 To make the sauce, gently whip the cream to floppy, limp peaks, then fold in the curd. Serve this cold over the warm pudding.

TROPICAL FRUIT PAVLOVA
SERVES 10–12

5 egg whites
285g sugar

For the topping
600ml double cream
5 kiwi fruits, peeled and sliced
200g raspberries
200g strawberries,
  hulled and halved
200g blueberries
Flesh from half a mango,
  in 1cm cubes
3 passionfruit, pulp only
Icing sugar to dust (optional)

Essential equipment
Large baking sheet, lined
  with baking paper
Piping bag with a large
  star nozzle

My mum has to be the best Pavlova maker in the world. Since I was a tiny tot she has made the gooiest, fluffiest meringue ever, and she isn't one to faff about either – she adds nothing but egg white and sugar, and lets the oven do the work. She makes a Pavlova every year for the Christmas dinner table and it truly does bring a moment of serenity to the end of a rowdy family feast. In fact this is one of the first baking ratios she ever taught me: 2oz sugar to every large egg white. This recipe is dedicated to you, Mum. I love you.

1 Preheat the oven to 180°C/Gas 4. Draw an A4 rectangle (using a piece of A4 paper as a guide) on the baking paper that lines the baking sheet. This will be the size of your meringue.

2 To make the meringue, place the egg whites in a large, metal mixing bowl and whisk using a hand-held electric mixer to stiff peaks. Many people whisk the whites to medium peaks and then add the sugar, but I find it better to add the sugar only when the whites are stiff. Continuing whisking on a medium speed and add the sugar a tablespoon at a time, whisking for 5 seconds or so after each addition and resisting the temptation to hurry the process. Once the sugar is well incorporated, your meringue should be stiff and very glossy.

CONTINUED OVERLEAF

3 Spoon two-thirds of the meringue on to the baking paper and spread into the A4 shape. Put the remaining meringue in the piping bag and pipe little peaks all the way round the edge of the meringue.

4 Place the meringue in the oven and immediately reduce the temperature to 130°C/Gas ½. Bake for 75 minutes, then turn off the oven but leave the meringue inside for at least 2 hours, or preferably overnight, with the door slightly ajar.

5 To make the topping, whisk the cream to soft, floppy peaks and spoon over the meringue. I only do this minutes before serving so that the meringue stays crispy and chewy. Place the prepared fruits on top, dribbling the pulp of the passionfruit over last. Finish with a sifting of icing sugar, if you like.

TIP
Plastic bowls tend to hang on to grease and fats, whereas metal bowls are easier to clean and are therefore better for making meringue. To ensure total cleanliness of the metal bowl, dab a little kitchen roll in vodka and wipe the insides of the bowl with it.

LEMON AND POPPY SEED SCONES
MAKES 10

100g natural yoghurt
120ml milk
1 tsp lemon juice
250g self-raising flour
250g strong white flour,
   plus extra for dusting
10g baking powder
100g caster sugar
125g salted butter
50g poppy seeds
Zest of 2 lemons
2 eggs
1 egg, beaten with a tiny
   pinch of salt, to glaze

Essential equipment
7.5cm/3-inch round cookie
   cutter, plain or fluted
Baking sheet, greased

The zesty flavour of these scones melts in the mouth and shouts summer at your taste buds. These are great with loosely whipped cream, butter and a good dollop of lemon curd.

1 Preheat the oven to 220°C/Gas 7.

2 Mix together the yoghurt, milk and lemon juice, and place to one side.

3 Put the flours, baking powder and sugar into a large mixing bowl. Cube the butter and rub it into the flour mixture until the mixture resembles breadcrumbs. Stir in the poppy seeds and lemon zest before adding the eggs and rubbing through into clumpy breadcrumbs.

4 Slowly add the yoghurt and milk mixture, mixing with a spoon or your hands, until the mixture is like a soft but fairly firm bread dough. Turn out of the bowl and gently push together for 30 seconds or so, then flatten out into a disc about 1.5cm thick. Cut out scones using the floured cookie cutter and place on a greased baking sheet.

5 Glaze the tops with beaten egg (do not glaze the sides as this will prevent the scones from rising) and bake for 13–15 minutes, or until golden brown and the scones sound hollow when tapped on the base.

CHAPTER SIX

MEMOIRS OF A BAKER

Baking is not just a love of mine, it's an inheritance. I bake because it has become part of my very nature to do so, and because the process brings with it exquisite tastes and smells, all of which have memories attached to them. It is these memories that so often act as the impetus for me to get into the kitchen and bake. If I am wallowing in nostalgia, I always want more than just the memory; I want the taste and the smell of it too. I think perhaps a major reason why I began to bake more while away from home – as well as the intrinsic therapy it provided – was because it reminded me of my family.

When I go to my family home and bake, my little nephew Harry loves to pop on his apron and bake alongside me. This gives me great comfort because I know that he will always remember that time we spent together, whenever he tastes a certain cake or smells a certain loaf of bread. Baking is the creation of memories.

ENGLISH MUFFINS
MAKES 10–12

500g strong white flour,
   plus extra for dusting
50g salted butter, diced
10g fast-action yeast
10g salt
50ml lager
50ml milk
170ml water
30ml cider vinegar

Essential equipment
9cm/3½-inch plain
   round cookie cutter
Baking sheet

I think my parents realized just how much I love cooking the first time I made eggs benedict. I remember the impressed look on my stepdad's face as I served him the plate of English muffins topped with poached eggs and a delicious hollandaise sauce. Whenever I bake these English muffins now, I think about that Sunday breakfast some years ago. It was wintertime and the log fire was lit. As the muffins were baking in Mum's Aga, I sat in front of it and placed my feet on one of its doors to keep me warm. I had been away all week at university and as I sat there, relaxing, with the smell of fresh muffins seeping out of the Aga, I realized that I wanted to bake for a living and not just for fun. So these, for me, represent more than just a simple English muffin: they were the breakfast over which I decided I would take a stab at changing my career.

1 Put the flour in a large mixing bowl and rub in the butter with your thumb and fingertips until well incorporated. Stir in the yeast, then the salt.

2 Pour the lager, milk and water into a small saucepan and heat until just warm but not hot – you need to be able to hold your finger in it without wanting to snatch it away. Add the cider vinegar, then pour this into the dry ingredients. Bring together into a rough dough using a wooden spoon, then turn out on to the worktop and knead until it is smooth and elastic – this takes about 10 minutes by hand. If you have one, you can knead for about 6 minutes in a freestanding electric mixer with a dough hook attachment.

CONTINUED OVERLEAF

ENGLISH MUFFINS
CONTINUED

3 Once the dough is kneaded, place it in an oiled bowl, cover with a damp tea towel or cling film, and leave to rise for 1 hour or until doubled in size.

4 Once the dough has doubled in size, tip it out and roll it out to about 1.5cm thick. Using the cookie cutter, cut out 10–12 muffins-to-be. Put these on a well-floured worktop, cover with a damp tea towel and leave for another hour or until just about doubled in volume.

5 Preheat the oven to 200°C/Gas 6. Place a non-stick frying pan on a medium heat. When the pan is hot, place 3 or 4 muffins in it – as many as you can fit in without crowding – and fry on one side for 2 minutes or until golden, then flip over and fry for a further minute or so until golden on the other side. Place on the baking sheet and put in the preheated oven for 10 minutes. Repeat with the remaining muffins.

6 When you remove the baked muffins from the oven, wrap them immediately in a barely damp tea towel – it mustn't be soaking wet otherwise it will ruin the muffins – so that they soften. I love these cut open and toasted with a good smearing of butter; they also make the perfect bread for a bacon sandwich with a good dollop of brown sauce.

APPLE, THYME AND PORK SAUSAGE ROLLS
MAKES 8

250g pork loin, diced
100g smoked bacon lardons
1 tsp salt
1 tsp black pepper
1 small Granny Smith apple,
  peeled, cored and roughly
  chopped
1 small brown onion,
  peeled and quartered
¼ tsp ground nutmeg
4 sprigs of thyme
1 tbsp wholegrain mustard
1 quantity Rough Puff Pastry
  (see page 22) or 500g shop-
  bought all-butter puff pastry
Flour for dusting
1 egg, beaten with a tiny
  pinch of salt, for glazing

Essential equipment
Food processor
Baking sheet lined with
  baking paper

Call me a big kid, but I love sausage rolls, and they remind me of a rare childhood treat. These are the perfect size for a grab-and-go lunch or supper, but if you wanted to serve them at a dinner party, you could slice each one into 6 smaller rolls and serve them as canapés.

1 Preheat the oven to 200°C/Gas 6.

2 Put the pork loin, lardons, salt, pepper, apple, onion, nutmeg, thyme and mustard into a food processor and pulse until everything is finely chopped and well mixed together. Set this sausage meat to one side until needed.

3 On a floured worktop and with a floured rolling pin, roll the pastry out to a rectangle of 30x36cm. Remember to move the pastry about after each roll to prevent it from sticking to the worktop. Cut the pastry into 8 rectangles of 15x9cm.

4 Take an eighth of the sausage meat and roll it into a thin sausage about 15cm long, then place this down the length of one pastry rectangle. Repeat with the remaining filling and pastry. Glaze the edges of the pastry with the beaten egg before rolling it around the filling. Place each roll on the baking sheet, well spaced to allow the pastry space to puff up, then glaze the top of each one with more egg. Score each roll 3 times diagonally across the top with a sharp knife, then bake for 30 minutes, or until the pastry is golden brown and puffed up.

DEEP FILLED APPLE PIES

MAKES 4

2 quantities of Shortcrust
   Pastry (see page 20),
   plus flour for dusting
7 Granny Smith apples
6 tbsp light brown
   muscovado sugar,
   plus extra for sprinkling
50g unsalted butter
1 egg, beaten with a tiny
   pinch of salt, for glazing

Essential equipment
4×180ml/6fl oz pudding
   moulds, greased

For me an apple pie has to be a deep one, otherwise it isn't worth having. I also like my apple pies to be unadulterated by spices or salt, and so these are simply apple and sugar. As a young lad, I used to devour packet after packet of apple pies secretly in my room. Now, being a baker, I make my own and these are so much better.

1 Preheat the oven to 200°C/Gas 6. Make the pastry as described on page 20. On a floured worktop using a floured rolling pin, roll the pastry out to about 4mm thick. Cut out 4 circles that are large enough to line the base and insides of the moulds, with a little excess to hang over. Line the pudding moulds with these pastry circles, pressing well down inside, then chill in the fridge for 30 minutes. Set the remaining pastry to one side for later.

2 Peel and core the apples, and cut into 5mm chunks.

3 Place the sugar and butter in a frying pan over a medium heat and allow to melt together, then add half of the apples. Cook until the apples squash when pressed with a spoon – about 10 minutes. Add the remaining apples and cook until just soft but with a little bite – about 5 minutes. Remove from the heat.

4 Fill the pastry-lined pudding moulds with the apple and sugar mix right to the top. With the remaining pastry, cut out circular lids. Glaze the edges of the pies with the beaten egg, place the lids on and jab a little hole in each pie. Crimp the lids to the sides with a fork, then trim off excess pastry with a sharp knife.

5 Glaze the tops of the pies with more egg, and sprinkle over a little more sugar. Bake for 35–40 minutes or until the pastry is a dark golden brown. Remove from the oven and allow to cool completely before taking out of the moulds. You can reheat these to eat them warm, but I have to eat them cold.

CHOCOLATE AND PEAR LONG TART

1 quantity Shortcrust Pastry
(see page 20), chilled for
30 minutes
415g tin pear halves
(about 5 pear halves)
Icing sugar, to sprinkle

For the frangipane
115g salted butter,
at room temperature
115g caster sugar
2 eggs
90g ground almonds
25g cocoa powder

Essential equipment
35×12cm/14×5-inch tarte
maison tin, preferably with
a loose base, or a 23–25cm/
9–10-inch round, loose-
bottomed flan tin
Baking paper and beans/rice

By long tart I mean, of course, a tart baked in a tarte maison tin. But as a working-class lad from a family of 'mick' takers, I daren't call this a tarte maison for fear of my life. Chocolate and pears is a combination that speaks for itself: the after-dinner treat made by Granny, or the only thing on the school dinner menu worth looking forward to. Whatever your happy memories of chocolate and pear, I hope this creates even more.

1 Preheat the oven to 200°C/Gas 6. Roll out the pastry and use to line the tart tin, pressing well into the grooves and leaving a flap of pastry over the edge, which can be trimmed off later. Prick the base all over with a fork and place in the freezer for 15 minutes.

2 Line the pastry with a sheet of baking paper, and fill with baking beans or rice. Blind-bake with the beans for 15 minutes, then remove the beans and paper, and bake for a further 12 minutes. Remove from the oven and allow to cool, and reduce the oven temperature to 180°C/Gas 4.

3 While the pastry case is baking, make the chocolate frangipane by beating together the butter and sugar until paler in colour and lighter in texture, then add the eggs and mix in. Add the ground almonds and cocoa powder and fold into a thick batter.

4 Pipe or spoon the frangipane into the tart case, leaving a good centimetre of pastry at the top. Top with the pear halves in a line down the length of the tart. If using a round tart tin, simply place the pears around the edges, or however you like. Sprinkle the pears with a little icing sugar, and bake for 25–35 minutes, or until the frangipane has puffed up around the pears. Sprinkle with a little more icing sugar to serve (see overleaf).

RHUBARB, GINGER AND CUSTARD ÉCLAIRS
MAKES 14

1 quantity Crème Pâtissière
(see page 24)

For the conserve
300g rhubarb chunks
(fresh or frozen is fine)
175g caster sugar
60ml sparkling wine
or Cava (optional)
2 balls of stem ginger

For the éclair shells
1 quantity Choux Pastry
(see page 23)

For the topping
200g chocolate (I use milk
but dark would work, too)

Essential equipment
2 baking sheets greased
with butter and put in
the fridge to set
Piping bags with 2cm plain
and number 2 nozzles
Piece of card cut to 10cm long
Flour for dusting

I couldn't write a chapter on the nostalgia of baking and not include something to do with rhubarb and custard. It is a classic flavour combo and I for one am unwilling to let it slip from our hands as our cuisine evolves. Making rhubarb and ginger conserve for this may seem like a lot to ask, but I promise you it really is just a matter of throwing some ingredients into a pan and waiting for the magic to happen. Crème pâtissière, while not the lumpy, Sunday-afternoon kind of custard, is custard all the same.

1 Make the crème pâtissière according to the recipe on page 24 and allow to cool completely.

2 Make the conserve by placing the rhubarb in a medium saucepan with the sugar, and wine, if using. Rinse the stem ginger balls under cold water to remove the sticky syrup, then finely grate into the pan. Set over a high heat and stir until everything begins to bubble. Reduce the heat slightly and allow the pan to simmer, quite roughly, stirring every few minutes, for about 15–20 minutes, or until most of the excess moisture has evaporated away and you are left with a loose, fruity conserve. Allow to cool completely.

3 Preheat the oven to 200°C/Gas 6.

4 Make the choux pastry according to the recipe on page 23. Use it to fill a piping bag fitted with a 2cm plain nozzle. Take the baking sheets from the fridge and, using the 10cm card dipped in flour, make 7 well-spaced parallel lines on each sheet. Pipe 10cm lines of choux, following the marks you've made. If you end up with little peaks at the end of each line, dampen your finger or a butter knife and push it into a uniform shape.

5 Bake the choux pastry for 20 minutes, then reduce the temperature to 180°C/Gas 4 and bake for a further 10–15 minutes. Turn off the oven and open the door slightly, but leave the éclairs in there to dry a little – they need to be crisp so they don't turn soggy when you add the filling.

6 Once the éclairs have cooled in the oven, remove them and slice each one in half horizontally – like a razor clam. Fill a piping bag fitted with the 2cm plain nozzle with the crème pâtissière and pipe a generous line of this into one half of each éclair. Spoon a heaped teaspoonful of the conserve on top of the crème pâtissière. Place the empty halves on top of the filling and line up on a cooling rack, with a piece of baking paper underneath the rack.

7 Chop the chocolate finely and place in a heatproof bowl. Set over a pan of barely simmering water and allow the chocolate to melt slowly, stirring every few moments to ensure an even temperature. Once melted, allow to cool for a minute or two before spooning in random, zigzag patterns over the éclairs – you can do this in a piping bag fitted with a number 2 nozzle if you wish. Serve the éclairs immediately, or store in the fridge until needed.

CRANBERRY, ORANGE AND MACADAMIA NUT BUNS WITH A STICKY BOOZY GLAZE

MAKES 12

For the bread
500g strong white flour
10g salt
10g caster sugar
10g fast-action yeast
200ml tepid water
100ml milk
1 egg
40g salted butter,
   at room temperature
Flavourless oil

For the filling and glaze
50g salted butter, softened
100g dark brown soft sugar
100g macadamia nuts, bashed
   in a bag with a rolling pin
   to small chunks
100g dried cranberries
Zest of 2 medium oranges
70g icing sugar
35ml water
35ml orange liqueur, such
   as Triple Sec or Cointreau

Essential equipment
Dough scraper
Deep roasting tray about
   23×30cm/9×12 inches

The Chelsea bun plays a part in everyone's history, I imagine. Any good bakery worth its salt sells batch upon batch of these treats every day. My version is sticky, crunchy, boozy and delicious.

1 To make the dough, place the flour in a bowl and stir in the salt and sugar. Add the yeast and stir it through the flour.

2 In a jug, beat together the water, milk and egg, then add half to the flour, mixing well with a fork. Slowly add the remaining liquid, then the softened butter. Using your hands, squeeze the dough in the bowl for a minute or so.

3 Turn the contents of the bowl out on to the worktop and knead for 10 minutes, or until the dough is smooth and elastic, and when you press a floured finger into it, the dent disappears. The dough will be wet, but try not to incorporate any more flour – you don't want the bread to be tough. Use a dough scraper to knead the dough if you find this easier.

4 Drizzle about 2 tablespoons of flavourless oil into a clean bowl, roll the dough in it so it is well oiled, then cover the bowl with cling film and leave to rise in a warmish place for 1 hour, or until doubled in size.

CRANBERRY, ORANGE AND MACADAMIA NUT BUNS WITH A STICKY BOOZY GLAZE
CONTINUED

5 After an hour, tip the dough out on to a floured worktop and roll into a rectangle of about 30×32cm – keep moving the dough around so that it doesn't stick to the surface. Spread the butter on the dough, then sprinkle with the sugar, macadamia nuts, cranberries and zest.

6 Roll the dough up tightly from the longer edge. Trim the ends, then slice using a sharp knife, or serrated bread knife, into 12 equal discs. Arrange these in 4 rows of 3 in the deep roasting tray. Cover with cling film then allow to rise for a second time for 45 minutes.

7 Preheat the oven to 220°C/Gas 7. To make the glaze, put the icing sugar, water and liqueur in a small saucepan and place over a high heat. Bring to the boil, then reduce to a simmer for a minute or so.

8 After the second rising time, bake the buns for 20 minutes or until nicely browned on top. As soon as you remove them from the oven, brush liberally with two-thirds of the glaze, then remove from the tray and place on a wire rack to cool.

9 Allow to cool completely before separating the buns and brushing with a final smothering of boozy glaze.

COCONUT AND CHOCOLATE MACAROONS
MAKES 12

150g desiccated coconut
125g caster sugar
2 egg whites
Seeds from 1 vanilla pod,
   or 1 tsp vanilla paste
   or extract
50g flour
100g milk chocolate

Essential equipment
Baking sheet, greased

How can any recipe chapter on nostalgia not include coconut macaroons? It would be like rewriting your family tree. When I was a young boy, my cousin and I used to play on my granddad's farm for hours and hours on end. At lunch time we would go to the local bakery with my auntie Frances, where there would always be an abundance of sweet-smelling coconut macaroons. I never quite had the courage to ask for one, though, and so I always ended up with the generic, though perfectly delicious, iced finger. Luckily for my auntie Frances, I now make these all the time and so I can let go of any grudges. These are great for making with kids.

1 Preheat the oven to 180°C/Gas 4.

2 Simply place all the ingredients, except the milk chocolate, in a bowl and mix with your hands into a sticky, gritty dough. It might look at first like the mixture won't come together, but it will. This is a very good job for small (clean) hands!

3 Scoop a heaped teaspoon of the dough out of the bowl and roll up in the palm of your hand to form a loose ball. Place on the baking sheet, and continue to make the rest of the macaroons in the same way. Bake for 15–20 minutes, or until golden brown. Leave to cool on a cooling rack.

4 Melt the milk chocolate and spoon, drizzle or simply throw it over the macaroons.

VARIATION
To jazz these up somewhat, try adding 100g chopped dried apricot to the macaroon mix. This will make them extra chewy.

APRICOT AND GINGER UPSIDE-DOWN CAKE
SERVES 8–12

7–8 apricots
200g caster sugar and
  1 tbsp water, for the caramel
115g salted butter,
  at room temperature
115g golden caster sugar
2 eggs
115g self-raising flour
30g ground almonds
2 tbsp milk
2 balls stem ginger,
  finely chopped
1 tbsp syrup from the
  stem ginger jar
½ tsp ground ginger

Essential equipment
20cm/8-inch loose-bottomed
  cake tin, greased and lined

An upside-down cake is not just a 1970s throwback, but rather a delicious, comforting and homely treat, ideal for a Sunday afternoon. The apricots bake into a sort of jam, and their sharpness is the perfect complement to the gentle, spicy ginger, and the sweet, almost pudding-like sponge.

1 Preheat the oven to 170°C/Gas 3.

2 Halve the apricots and remove their stones.

3 Mix the sugar and water for the caramel in a medium saucepan, then place over a high heat. Bring to the boil, remembering not to stir the pan at any point (or you'll end up with crystallized rather than caramelized sugar). When the caramel is amber and the bubbles are subsiding, remove and quickly pour into the lined tin.

4 Arrange the apricot halves on the caramel, being careful not to burn your fingers because, believe me, it hurts.

5 To make the cake, cream together the butter and sugar until paler in colour and lighter in texture. (Easiest with an electric whisk or in a freestanding mixer.) Add the eggs, one at a time, and incorporate gently. Then sift in the flour and almonds and fold into the mixture, along with the milk, stem ginger, syrup and ground ginger.

6 Pour this batter on top of the caramel and apricots. Bake for around 30 minutes, or until golden brown and a skewer inserted into the centre comes out clean – remember that there may still be bits of soft fruit stuck to the knife, which is fine.

7 Place a large plate upside down on top of the cake tin. Using oven gloves to protect from the heat, swiftly turn the cake-and-plate combo upside down and tap the tin to help the cake fall. Remove the tin and baking paper and voila: a perfect upside-down cake.

CHERRY AND CHOC ROLY POLY PUDDING

SERVES 6–8

For the pastry
250g self-raising flour
75g caster sugar
30g salted butter, cubed,
  plus extra for greasing
100g shredded suet
150ml milk

For the filling
100g black cherry jam
75g milk chocolate chips
100g fresh cherries,
  pitted and roughly chopped

Custard, cream or ice cream,
  to serve

Essential equipment
Large baking sheet, baking
  paper and aluminium foil

I know this is incredibly old-fashioned and probably verging on immature, but I refuse to feel ashamed. Sometimes all I crave is a dessert from my childhood, drowned in custard. What can be so shameful about that?

1 To make the pastry, stir the flour and sugar together in a bowl, then add the butter and rub in until well incorporated. Add the suet and stir in well. Pour in two-thirds of the milk and, using your hands, bring the pastry together. Add the remaining milk and squeeze the pastry together well. Turn out on to the counter top and knead gently for a minute or so, just until the suet is well distributed.

2 Preheat the oven to 180°C/Gas 4. Take the baking sheet and line it with aluminium foil, then place a large piece of baking paper on the foil. Grease the baking paper with butter. The paper and foil will be used to wrap the roly poly.

3 Roll out the suet pastry to a rough rectangle about the size of an A3 piece of paper. Spread the jam over the entire surface of the pastry, then sprinkle the chocolate chips and chopped cherries all over. Roll the pastry up tightly from the shortest edge to make a nice, fat, jammy roly poly. Place this, seam-side down, on the greased baking paper and wrap that around it. Then wrap the foil loosely around the paper-wrapped pudding, leaving room for it to expand as it cooks. Bake for 1 hour.

4 Serve hot with custard, cream or ice cream.

AUNTIE MARY'S LEMON CURD CAKE

SERVES 6

150g self-raising flour
125g salted butter,
   at room temperature
125g caster sugar
2 eggs
2 tbsp home-made Lemon
   Curd (see page 26) or
   best quality shop-bought
1 lemon, zest and juice

Essential equipment
1lb (450g) loaf tin, greased
   and lined with baking paper

I loved my auntie Mary. She was a stern woman but she enjoyed a good joke. The day of her funeral was the day I had to collect my A-Level results and so I didn't say goodbye to her. I regret this, and since then I have always vowed that family comes first. This is dedicated to you, Auntie Mary – you are deeply missed but merrily remembered.

1 Preheat the oven to 180°C/Gas 4.

2 Place the flour, butter, sugar – keeping back 3 teaspoonfuls – eggs, lemon curd and lemon zest in a large mixing bowl – or freestanding electric mixer – and beat together gently into a smooth batter. Pour this into the prepared tin and bake for 20–25 minutes.

3 Mix the lemon juice with the reserved caster sugar. Remove the baked cake from the oven and immediately pour the sweetened lemon juice over it. Allow the cake to stand in the tin for at least 20 minutes, then transfer to a wire rack to cool.

STRAWBERRY AND CUSTARD SHORTBREADS
MAKES 12

For the biscuits
250g plain flour,
  plus extra for dusting
50g Bird's custard powder
100g caster sugar
200g salted butter,
  cut into 1cm cubes

*For the cream and
strawberry topping*
200ml double cream
20 small strawberries
2 tbsp caster sugar

Essential equipment
5cm/2-inch cookie cutter
Baking sheet

Strawberries, custard and cream remind me of my youth. I don't miss my youth all that much, but I do like to revel in memories every once in a while. These thick discs of crumbling custard shortbread with piles of floppy cream topped with macerated strawberries are delicious at any time of the day (see overleaf). They look particularly grand stacked on a cake tier and served with pots of posh tea.

1 Preheat the oven to 180°C/Gas 4.

2 Place the flour, custard powder and sugar in a mixing bowl and stir together briefly. Add the cubes of butter and rub into the dry mixture using your thumb and fingers, until the butter is well incorporated and you have a sandy mixture. Bring the mixture together with your hands, grabbing and squeezing the crumbs until they start to clump together, then tip the contents on to the worktop and knead for a minute or two until the mixture comes together like pastry and you are able to roll it out. Leave to rest in the fridge for 15 minutes.

3 Meanwhile, whip the cream until it forms soft, floppy peaks, and place to one side.

4 Remove the stalks and leaves from the strawberries and quarter each one. Place the chopped strawberries in a mixing bowl and toss with the sugar. Allow the strawberries to macerate in the sugar – this means the sugars will draw out some of the natural fruit juices and create a thick, syrupy coating on the fruit.

5 After allowing the shortbread dough to rest, lightly flour the worktop and a rolling pin, and roll the dough out into a disc about 1cm thick. Cut out circles of shortbread using the cutter and place on the baking sheet. Make sure you leave a good inch between each circle as they will spread slightly as they bake.

6 Slide the baking sheet into the oven and allow the shortbread discs to bake for 20–25 minutes, or until lightly browned around the edges. Remove from the oven and recut each disc with the cookie cutter, as quick as you can before they harden. Save the trimmings in a little bowl to crumble and sprinkle over the tops later.

7 Allow the baked, re-cut shortbread discs to cool completely, before dolloping a tablespoon of cream on to each, then topping that with a spoonful of macerated strawberries and, if you like, a sprinkle of the crumbled shortbread trimmings.

BLACK CHERRY DOUGHNUTS
MAKES 10

500g strong white flour
10g salt
50g caster sugar
7g fast-action yeast (1 sachet)
240ml milk
40g unsalted butter
2 eggs

For the filling and coating
370g best quality black
  cherry jam
3 tbsp kirsch or crème
  de cassis (optional)
150g caster sugar

Essential equipment
Dough scraper
Deep-fat fryer or large
  saucepan filled with
  3 litres sunflower oil
Pastry syringe

Doughnuts have to be one of the most comforting foods to eat – I love the tickle of the sugar on my lips, and the smell transports me to the funfairs and fêtes of my childhood. These ones are a little bit grown-up, however – the addition of kirsch to the jam makes them an adult treat. Black cherry jam is my favourite, but you are free to fill these with whatever you like – maybe even an oozing of chocolate ganache. These are best eaten on the day they are made, but they will be fine for a couple of days if stored in an airtight container in the fridge.

1 First make a simple, enriched bread dough. Put the flour in a large mixing bowl and stir the salt and sugar into it, then add the yeast.

2 Put the milk and butter in a saucepan over a medium heat and warm up until you can just hold your finger in the milk without needing to snatch it back quickly. Mix well so the butter melts, then add the eggs and beat them in.

3 Slowly add the liquid ingredients to the dry ingredients, mixing them together with a dough scraper or wooden spoon. When the liquid has been incorporated, tip the contents of the bowl out on to the worktop and knead for 10 minutes. The mixture will be extremely sticky, so the best way to knead it is by picking it up and slamming it on to the counter top, then folding it over. This is why a dough scraper is a great tool. If you have a freestanding electric mixer with dough hook attachment, it might be easier to knead the dough in that for 5 minutes on low.

CONTINUED OVERLEAF

BLACK CHERRY DOUGHNUTS CONTINUED

4 When the dough is smooth and elastic, place it in a floured bowl and cover with a damp cloth. Leave to rise for 1 hour.

5 After the dough has risen, weigh it into 10 equal pieces (around 86g each). Roll these pieces into perfect balls, place on a floured baking sheet or board well spaced apart, and cover in cling film to rise again for 45 minutes.

6 Meanwhile, put the jam into a saucepan, with the kirsch or crème de cassis if using, and heat just until the jam is runny. Sieve the jam into a bowl to remove any bits of cherry skin.

7 Pour the caster sugar on a plate and place next to the deep-fat fryer, alongside a cooling rack.

8 Fifteen minutes before the dough balls are ready, heat the deep-fat fryer to 180°C. Test the heat of the oil (if you don't have a thermometer) by dropping a cube of bread into it; if it sizzles, the oil is ready. Fry the doughnuts 2 or 3 at a time, for about 3–4 minutes per side. Remove from the fryer using a slotted spoon, dip in the sugar and coat well, then place on the rack.

9 Put the jam into the syringe. Inject each doughnut with a little jam, aiming to get it in the centre. If jam starts to ooze out, simply dip the hole into the caster sugar and stand the doughnut up so the hole is on top. Devour.

BAKEWELL MUFFINS
MAKES 12

225g plain flour
2 tsp baking powder
150g caster sugar
150g glacé cherries,
  roughly chopped
225ml milk
2 eggs
115g salted butter, melted
1 tsp almond extract

Essential equipment
12-hole deep muffin tray,
  lined with paper cases

I adore the old cherry and almond combination. The flavour is so reminiscent of childhood that it takes me back immediately.

1 Preheat the oven to 180°C/Gas 4.

2 Put the flour, baking powder, sugar and chopped cherries in a mixing bowl and stir together.

3 In a jug, whisk together the milk, eggs, melted butter and almond extract, then slowly pour this into the bowl containing the dry ingredients. Fold together, but don't over-mix (you don't want the muffin texture to be tough), then divide the batter between the muffin cases.

4 Gently tap the muffin tray down on the worktop 3 or 4 times to expel any large air bubbles. Bake for 25–30 minutes, or until the muffins are well risen and golden brown. Allow to cool, then enjoy.

COFFEE AND WALNUT PRALINE CHOUX RING

SERVES 6–8

1 quantity Choux Pastry
  (see page 23)
400ml double cream
6 tbsp icing sugar
2 tbsp freeze-dried coffee
  dissolved in 2 tbsp hot water
250g mascarpone cheese
150g caster sugar and
  1 tbsp water
100g walnut pieces

For the icing
125g icing sugar and
  about ½ tbsp water

Essential equipment
2 baking sheets lined
  with baking paper
Piping bags with 2cm
  and large star nozzles

Coffee and walnut has to be the ultimate in retro recipe flavours, but it is one that has survived many food evolutions, and I genuinely believe is here to stay. When I made a coffee and walnut cake for my family, my nephew, Harry, ate endless slices of it, and because of the caffeine he wouldn't go to sleep that evening and made his parents' night a misery. The moral of this story is: if you're going to serve this to children, it might be wise to use decaffeinated coffee.

1 Preheat the oven to 200°C/Gas 6. Draw a 25cm circle on the baking paper on one of the baking sheets, using a dinner plate or flan ring.

2 Make the choux pastry according to the recipe on page 23. Use it to fill a piping bag fitted with the 2cm plain nozzle. Pipe a ring of choux pastry on the baking sheet, following the line of the circle you drew. Then pipe another ring directly next to it, on the inside. Finally, pipe a third ring of choux on top of the first two, using the line where they meet as a guide.

3 Bake for 30–35 minutes, or until dark golden – choux pastry needs to be fairly bronzed in order for it to be crisp, but don't let it burn. Remove from the oven and allow to cool completely.

CONTINUED OVERLEAF

COFFEE AND WALNUT PRALINE CHOUX RING
CONTINUED

4 While the choux ring bakes, make the filling by whipping the cream in a mixing bowl to soft, floppy peaks. Gently mix in the icing sugar and dissolved coffee, along with the mascarpone – it will thicken considerably, but that's what we want.

5 Make the praline by mixing the caster sugar with the water in a medium saucepan. Place it over a high heat. Boil until the sugar caramelizes and turns a golden amber colour – remember not to stir at any point once the heat is on, otherwise you'll end with a pan of sugar crystals. Remove the amber caramel from the heat, throw in the walnuts, swirl the pan around to coat the walnuts, then tip on to the second lined baking sheet and allow to set completely.

6 Once the choux ring is cool, using a bread knife, slice it in half horizontally so you end up with 2 choux rings – don't worry if it breaks a bit, you can strategically disguise that later. Put the filling in a piping bag fitted with a large star nozzle and pipe on to the base choux ring – I tightly zigzag the filling into the ring.

7 Peel the baking paper from the solidified praline, and place it on a chopping board. Using a sharp knife, chop it into small chunks – you could just blitz it in a food processor, but don't blitz it to crumbs as you still want a few chunky, chewy bits of caramelized walnut. Sprinkle three-quarters of the chopped praline on to the filling, pressing it gently in so that it stays in place. Place the top half of the choux ring on the filling.

8 Make the icing by mixing together the icing sugar and water. Add the water slowly, stirring constantly, until you have a thick but runny icing – you may need less or more water, depending on the absorbency of the icing sugar. Once ready, drizzle the icing on top of the choux ring, coaxing some of it to drip seductively down the edges. Finish with a scattering of the remaining chopped praline.

CHAPTER SEVEN
SIMPLE SPEEDY SOLUTIONS

I completely endorse the odd lazy day, and I am not afraid to admit that, every once in a while, I spend the entire day in my pyjamas. If I stay with my family, however, I am never allowed to stay in bed past 7 a.m. My mum and stepdad are farmers and get up every morning at 5 a.m. to milk the cows. As a teenager my job was to feed the calves and so I too was plucked from slumber in the very early hours. Now that I have free rein of my schedules I sometimes – only sometimes, Mum – make up for those early mornings with a lazy day.

One thing I cannot abide, however, is letting my baking slip because I'm feeling lazy. Yes, I have lazy days, but I'm still incredibly greedy. So sometimes I like to bake things that are much quicker than my normal endeavours, or involve simpler or fewer stages.

SUNFLOWER SEED SODA BREAD
SERVES 8–10

330–350ml milk
1 tsp lemon juice
250g strong white flour
250g strong wholemeal flour
40g lard
200g sunflower seeds
2 tsp bicarbonate of soda
1½ tsp salt

Essential equipment
Baking sheet

Normal breads can take the best part of three hours to make, but sometimes I crave a slice of home-made bread and need to leave the house in a couple of hours. This recipe is perfect for when time is short, and it doesn't sacrifice any of the fantastic flavour.

1 Preheat the oven to 190°C/Gas 5.

2 Start the dough by putting the milk in a jug with the lemon juice and set to one side. Sift the flours into a mixing bowl; leave any bran in the sieve and keep it for later.

3 Cut the lard into 1cm chunks and rub into the flour. Mix the seeds, bicarbonate of soda and salt into the flour and lard, then slowly add the milk, squeezing the ingredients together as you go until you have a soft dough.

4 Tip the dough on to the worktop and gently push together; this isn't kneading so much as squashing the dough down, or 'chafing'. Leave the dough to rest for 10 minutes or so.

5 Shape the dough into a large ball, then, with the floured handle of a wooden spoon, make a large cross in the dough ball, almost cutting right through. Sprinkle the loaf with the reserved bran. Place on the baking sheet, then into the oven for 35–40 minutes, or until nicely browned with a crispy crust.

CORIANDER AND GARLIC FLATBREADS
MAKES 12

350g white bread flour,
  plus extra for dusting
150g wholemeal flour
  (doesn't have to be
  bread flour)
10g salt
2 tsp baking powder
50g unsalted butter,
  cut into cubes
150ml natural yoghurt
200ml freshly boiled water
50ml olive oil
Small handful fresh
  coriander, roughly torn
1 garlic clove, minced
  or finely chopped
Pinch of salt and pepper

Essential equipment
2 dinner plates to keep the
  flatbreads warm and soft

I love flavour, and sometimes I do go a little overboard with it, but these are just gorgeous, scented with coriander and garlic. Even better, they are very easy to make and handy to freeze in batches, then defrost to have as a last-minute accompaniment to dips and chilli con carne. They are delicious on their own, but I also stuff them with spinach, feta cheese, mint and pomegranate kernels for a Moroccan munch.

1 In a large bowl mix together the flours, salt and baking powder. Rub the butter into the flour mixture until well combined.

2 In a jug, whisk together the yoghurt and water, then slowly add to the dry ingredients. Bring the contents of the bowl together into a dough. Tip on to the worktop and knead the dough for a minute or until smooth. Allow to rest for a minute or two.

3 Meanwhile, preheat a frying pan over a high heat without any oil in it. Mix together the oil, coriander, garlic, salt and pepper in a small glass or cup.

4 Divide the dough into 12 balls of about 65g each. If you are busy, don't bother to weigh, just divide the ball into 2, then each half into 6. Flatten the balls out and, using plenty of flour, roll them into circles about 2mm thick. Place, one by one, on the hot pan. Fry for 1 minute on each side, or until bubbly and full of brown spots, then brush with the oil and store between two dinner plates so they steam and keep incredibly soft.

TIP
If you want to make just one or two, simply cut off and roll the desired amount, then wrap the rest in cling film and store in the fridge for up to 24 hours.

CHEESE AND CHIVE CORNBREAD BUNS

MAKES 10

300g instant polenta/cornmeal
½ tsp bicarbonate of soda
1 tsp salt
1 tsp ground black pepper
10g fresh chives,
    finely chopped
40g strong Cheddar cheese,
    finely grated
150ml milk
150ml lemonade
1 tbsp honey
2 eggs
130ml sunflower oil

Essential equipment
12-hole deep muffin tray,
    filled with 10 paper cases
    (leave 2 central holes free)

I adore cornbread. Whenever I do my barbecue pulled pork, or something equally Southern American, I always serve it alongside a mountain of cornbread muffins. Sometimes, though, if I want a quick and easy lunch, I will make a batch of these muffins to serve with cream cheese, and maybe even – if I'm feeling particularly sophisticated – a slice of smoked salmon or some finely sliced, roasted ham. The secret – if it can really be called that – is to use lemonade in these buns. Not only does it give a sweet-sharp flavour lift, but the bubbles work alongside the bicarbonate of soda to ensure the buns are wonderfully light and tender.

1 Preheat the oven to 180°C/Gas 4.

2 Put the polenta, bicarbonate of soda, salt, pepper, chives and cheese into a large mixing bowl. Place the milk, lemonade, honey, eggs and sunflower oil into a large jug and beat together. Add to the dry ingredients and mix gently and quickly until everything is evenly dispersed.

3 Gently fill the cases to barely a couple of millimetres from the top, then bake for 15–20 minutes. Allow to cool before serving.

CHEWY BREAKFAST BARS

MAKES 16

200g salted butter
150g light brown
   muscovado sugar
1 tbsp golden syrup
100g walnuts
100g Brazil nuts
100g dried dates
100g dried apricots
100g dried cranberries
150g porridge oats

Essential equipment
20×30cm/8×10-inch Swiss roll
   tin, lined with baking paper

These bars really are chewy. The dried fruits and buttery oats are the perfect contrast to the crunch of the nuts. They are simple to make; not necessarily fast, but simple nonetheless. What's more, they are even better made the night before and stored in an airtight tin ready for a nourishing, swift breakfast.

1 Preheat the oven to 180°C/Gas 4.

2 Place the butter, sugar and golden syrup in a saucepan over a medium heat and stir until the butter has melted and the sugar has dissolved into it.

3 Chop the walnuts and brazil nuts into rough chunks – I find it easiest to throw them in a sandwich bag and smash with a rolling pin or heavy jar. Chop the dried dates and apricots fairly finely. Put the nuts, fruits and oats into a large mixing bowl, then pour in the sugary butter, mixing with a wooden spoon until everything is well coated.

4 Scoop into the prepared tin and even out with the wooden spoon. Bake for 25 minutes.

5 Remove from the oven and allow to cool completely before turning out from the tin and slicing into 16 pieces.

APPLE AND OAT FRITTERS
MAKES 10

1 egg
60g plain flour
60g milk
30g instant oats
2 small Granny Smith apples,
   peeled and cored
1 tsp mixed spice
30g salted butter, melted
2 tbsp light brown
   muscovado sugar
sunflower oil for frying

I love apples and oats together. The earthy, straw-flavoured oats are just perfect with the tangy apples. These fritters are the work of minutes, so if you're in a lazy mood or simply rushing for breakfast, they are perfect. I love these with a dollop of thick Greek yoghurt, and a drizzle of honey.

1 Place a frying pan over a high heat and allow to warm up. Put the egg, flour, milk and oats in a bowl and whisk together. Coarsely grate the peeled apples in, then add the spice, butter and sugar, and mix well.

2 Place a little oil in the frying pan and reduce the heat to medium. Add tablespoonfuls of the mix, about 3 at a time depending on the size of the pan. Cook on one side for about a minute, before flipping over and cooking the other side for about 30 seconds, or until both sides are lightly browned. Serve at once.

FRUIT AND NUT CHOCOLATE TART

SERVES 8–12

1 quantity Shortcrust Pastry
(see page 20)
300g milk chocolate (or you
could use half milk, half
dark – as you prefer),
broken into squares
200ml double cream
30g salted butter
150g Brazil nuts,
chopped in half
150g dried raisins (but you
could use cranberries,
apricots, dates – whatever
you fancy)

Essential equipment
35×12cm/14×5-inch tarte
maison tin
Baking paper and beans
for blind-baking

This tart is so simple to make. Once you've made and baked the pastry case, it is a matter of melting chocolate and cream, and throwing in some fruit and nuts.

1 Preheat the oven to 200°C/Gas 6.

2 Roll the pastry out to about 3mm thick and use to line the tarte maison tin. Line with paper and baking beans and blind-bake for 15 minutes. Remove the paper and baking beans and return to the oven for a further 12 minutes. Remove and allow to cool completely. (See page 19 for more on how to blind-bake a pastry case perfectly.)

3 When the pastry case has cooled, place the chocolate squares, cream and butter in a saucepan over a low heat and allow to melt together, stirring constantly with a metal spoon. When you have a smooth chocolaty liquid, stir in the nuts and fruit, and pour into the pastry case. Place in the fridge, uncovered, and allow to set for at least 2 hours before serving.

SALTED PEANUT AND CHOCOLATE FLORENTINES MAKES ABOUT 12

For the florentines
60g unsalted butter
60g light brown
    muscovado sugar
2 tsp liquid glucose
4 dried apricots,
    finely chopped
150g salted peanuts,
    roughly crushed
1½ tbsp plain flour

For the topping
100g dark chocolate,
    broken up

Essential equipment
2 baking sheets lined
    with baking paper

Just because I'm in a hurry, doesn't mean I have to sacrifice flavour. And these florentines are the epitome of flavour. They are inspired by Nigella Lawson's Sweet and Salty Crunch Nut Bars, which are an absolute favourite in my house. So this recipe is dedicated to Nigella, who never fails to inspire me.

1 Preheat the oven to 180°C/Gas 4.

2 Place the butter, sugar and glucose in a small saucepan and set over a medium heat. Stir until everything has melted and mixed together. Remove the pan from the heat and add the remaining ingredients, stirring well until everything is well mixed and the peanuts and apricots are coated in the sweet, buttery syrup.

3 Dollop teaspoonfuls of the mixture on to the lined baking sheets, leaving large gaps between each blob to allow the florentines to spread as they bake.

4 Bake for 6–8 minutes. Remove from the oven and leave to cool on the baking sheets. Once cool, the florentines should be bronzed and hard. Gently peel the baking paper from them and line them up on a wire cooling rack, with a sheet of foil underneath to catch drips.

5 Melt the chocolate in a heatproof bowl over a pan of barely simmering water. Drizzle, pour or dollop this over the florentines and allow to set (see overleaf).

LAST-MINUTE FRUIT CAKE
SERVES 8–12

150g dried sweetened
 cranberries
250g dried seedless prunes,
 roughly chopped
250g glacé cherry halves
150g currants
175g dried seedless dates,
 roughly chopped
400ml Guinness or
 other stout
75ml brandy
225g dark brown
 muscovado sugar
225g salted butter
4 eggs, beaten
225g plain flour
200g walnuts, chopped
Zest of 1 large lemon
Zest of 1 large orange
150g mixed peel
2 tsp mixed spice

Essential equipment
23cm/9-inch loose-bottomed
 cake tin, greased and
 double-lined with paper
Circle of tin foil for the top
Baking sheet

There is very often a need for fruit cake, be it for Christmas, a christening or even just to answer a craving. I find that I make at least five a year. Sometimes, though, they are onerous as they require months of feeding. This recipe cuts out all of that, and you end up with a fruit cake moist enough to devour on the day of making. It is important to prepare the tin correctly. You need two layers of baking paper. Cut two circles for the base, then line the sides with two layers of paper that protrude above the tin by a good inch.

1 Preheat the oven to 140°C/Gas 1.

2 Place the cranberries, prunes, cherries, currants and dates in a large saucepan with the stout and set over a high heat. Bring to the boil and allow to bubble away for 1 minute, then reduce to a simmer and leave for about 5 minutes.

3 Remove from the heat and add the brandy, sugar and butter, and stir with a wooden spoon until well incorporated. Stir in the eggs and flour, along with the walnuts, zests, mixed peel and mixed spice. Mix well together, then scoop into the prepared tin. Gently cover the cake tin with the circle of foil, having cut a small hole in the centre: this will protect the top of the cake from burning.

4 Place the tin on a baking sheet and transfer to the oven. Bake for 3½–4 hours, or until the cake has stopped making a gentle bubbling, crackling sound. Remove from the oven and leave to cool completely in the tin before turning out on to a cake stand.

5 Decorate as the occasion demands.

BANOFILO PIE
SERVES 8

6 sheets of filo pastry
75g unsalted butter, melted
3 tbsp icing sugar mixed
   with 1 tsp mixed spice
6 large bananas
75g light brown
   muscovado sugar

To serve
400ml double cream
Seeds from 1 vanilla pod,
   or 1 tsp vanilla paste
   or extract
4 tbsp icing sugar

Essential equipment
Pastry brush
20cm/8-inch loose-
   bottomed cake tin

I have always been as much of a fiend for filo as I have for banoffee pie, so I thought I would bring the two together into this glorious creation. The filo can easily dry out, so it is best to cover it with a damp tea towel when you start, and take the sheets from under that.

1 Preheat the oven to 180°C/Gas 4.

2 Start by buttering up the filo. Take one sheet at a time and spread lots of butter all over it using the pastry brush, and then place it in the cake tin, leaving overhang all the way round. Sift some of the icing sugar and spice mix over this. Repeat with the remaining 5 sheets, buttering and icing them as you go, and placing each sheet of pastry into the tin at a right angle to the last, as if you are making a cross. Make sure you save a little butter and icing sugar for the top, too.

3 Slice the bananas into 5mm rounds and place in a mixing bowl with the muscovado sugar. Mix together with your hands, allowing the natural juices in the bananas to ooze into the sugar to create a gloopy coating. Pile the bananas into the filo-lined tin, then take the overhanging pastry and cover the bananas with it. You should have a filo-wrapped banana parcel. Paint the top with the remaining melted butter, and sprinkle with the remaining icing sugar-spice mix.

4 Bake for 30 minutes, or until golden brown and the pastry is crispy. Remove from the oven and allow to cool in the tin.

5 To serve, whisk the cream with the vanilla until very soft peaks form. Fold in the icing sugar, then blob this on to the cooled pie.

CHOUX BUNS WITH CHOCOLATE GANACHE
SERVES 4

1 quantity Choux Pastry
(see page 23)

For the crème Chantilly
1 litre double cream
6 tbsp icing sugar
Seeds from 3 vanilla pods,
   or 3 tsp vanilla paste
   or extract

For the ganache
250g milk chocolate, chopped
250ml single cream
50g unsalted butter

Essential equipment
Piping bags and 2cm
   and 1cm plain nozzles
1 large or 2 small baking
   sheets, greased

Sometimes the simplest of things give the greatest amount of pleasure. You don't have to fill these choux buns with crème Chantilly; you could use crème pâtissière instead, or even chocolate mousse. But this is my favourite, with chocolate ganache to drizzle on top.

1 Preheat the oven to 200°C/Gas 6.

2 Make the choux pastry according to the recipe on page 23 and use it to fill a piping bag fitted with a 2cm plain nozzle. Pipe 12 large blobs of about 5cm diameter on the greased baking sheet/s and bake the choux buns for 25 minutes. Remove from the oven, make a little steam hole in each one, and return to the oven for 10 minutes more. Finally, remove from the oven and allow to cool completely.

3 Put the double cream, icing sugar and vanilla in a large mixing bowl and whisk until the cream is soft but holds its shape. Use to fill a piping bag fitted with a 1cm plain nozzle. With a sharply pointed knife, cut a little X into each choux bun where you made the steam hole earlier, gently place the nozzle of the piping bag in this hole and fill the bun with cream. Place on individual plates, or tower them up on one large plate to serve as a show-stopping dessert.

4 Put the milk chocolate in a heatproof bowl. Warm the single cream in a saucepan over a medium heat until just too hot for you to hold your finger in it. Pour the cream over the chocolate and stir until it has melted and you have a smooth, slick sauce. Stir in the butter, then pour over the choux buns and serve.

CHOUX-ROS
MAKES
ABOUT 20

1/3 quantity Choux Pastry
    (see page 23)
100g sugar
2 tsp cinnamon

For the dipping sauce
100g milk chocolate
50ml cream
2 tbsp golden syrup

Equipment
Deep-fat fryer or large
    saucepan filled with
    2 litres sunflower oil
Piping bag and large
    star nozzle

It seems the greedy world has gone churros mad. The Spanish doughnut is a tasty treat, and simpler and quicker to make than the traditional yeast-leavened kind. If I'm feeling famished but fatigued, I'll make a batch of these. Many recipes mix flour and water together with a bit of bicarbonate, but I much prefer my version, which is made with choux pastry. The outside becomes really crisp when fried, but the inside is fluffy and delicate, so you won't have any trouble polishing off a batch of these.

1 Follow the recipe on page 23 to make the choux pastry. Place the sugar and cinnamon on a plate and mix together well.

2 Heat the deep-fat fryer or saucepan full of oil to about 180°C. You will know it's hot enough when a cube of bread sizzles noisily when dropped in. While it is heating, make the chocolate dipping sauce by melting the ingredients together in a pan over a low heat. Once completely melted and glossy, decant into a bowl ready for the choux-ros.

3 Once the oil is hot, fill the piping bag with the choux pastry. Squeeze 3cm sausages of choux and snip them off with scissors into the hot oil. Fry in batches, as you don't want to overcrowd the pan and reduce the heat. Allow to fry until golden brown, then remove them with a slotted spoon and roll them in the sugar and cinnamon mixture.

4 Serve immediately with the warm chocolate sauce.

ONE-MIX CARROT CAKE WITH ORANGE AND CREAM CHEESE FROSTING SERVES 12

For the cake
220ml sunflower oil
225g caster sugar
4 eggs
225g self-raising flour
1 tsp baking powder
150g juicy raisins
200g finely grated carrot,
   squeezed in a tea towel to
   remove surplus moisture
150g chopped mixed nuts
2 tsp mixed spice
Zest of 1 large orange
Zest of 1 lemon

For the frosting
80g salted butter,
   at room temperature
450g icing sugar, sifted
400g full-fat cream cheese
Zest of 2 oranges
Walnut halves and ground
   cinnamon, to finish

Essential equipment
2×20cm/8-inch sandwich
   tins, greased and lined

There isn't always time to cream butter and sugar, then slowly add eggs, before folding in flour. Sometimes I just need to make a cake, and quickly. This is the perfect cake for such an occasion (see overleaf).

1 Preheat the oven to 160°C/Gas 3.

2 Put all the ingredients for the cake in a large mixing bowl and combine, using a wooden spoon, into a smooth batter studded with carrot, raisins and nuts.

3 Divide between the 2 tins and bake for 30–40 minutes (switching the tins halfway through if you don't have room for both on the same shelf), or until golden brown and a skewer inserted into the centre comes out clean. Allow the cakes to cool completely, then slice each one through the middle into 2 discs.

4 To make the icing, put the butter and icing sugar in a bowl and rub the butter in as though you were making a crumble mix. Then add the cream cheese and orange zest and mix to a smooth frosting. If you have a food processor, simply put the ingredients in that and blitz to a smooth frosting.

5 Use the frosting to sandwich the layers of cake together, saving plenty for the top. Decorate with walnut halves and a sprinkle of ground cinnamon.

CHAPTER EIGHT

DEEPEST DARK DESIRES

I don't always bake just because I'm in a certain mood. Sometimes I have an incessant craving for something rich, dark and inviting, and so I bake because I am feeling particularly greedy. On cosy nights and Sunday afternoons, I think it is important to indulge a little bit – because really, if you can't have a treat every once in a while, you are being far too hard on yourself.

The recipes in this chapter are ones I make when luscious longings manifest themselves and I am ravenous for something rich. These are recipes that will satisfy – or at least help to satisfy – the greedy moments.

PESTO, BALSAMIC AND GARLIC BREAD
SERVES 10–12

400g strong white flour,
   plus extra for dusting
1 tsp salt
7g fast-action yeast (1 sachet)
280ml tepid water

For the garlic pesto butter
100g salted butter
4 large garlic cloves, finely
   chopped or crushed
1 tbsp green pesto

For the balsamic syrup
3 tbsp balsamic vinegar
1 tbsp caster sugar

To finish
3 tbsp freshly grated
   Parmesan cheese
Handful fresh basil leaves
Black pepper
Sea salt flakes

This is the ultimate feast dish, a giant platter of buttery garlic bread, sprinkled with pesto, balsamic, basil and Parmesan cheese. I created this to take to my sister's house to serve alongside her lasagne, but it was devoured before the main course was even cooked. The idea for this bread came from my lovely sister-in-law, Louise. Thank you, Louise.

1 Place the flour in a mixing bowl and stir in the salt, then the yeast. Slowly add the water to the flour, mixing into a messy dough. Turn out on to the worktop and knead for about 10 minutes until smooth and elastic. Alternatively, make the dough in a freestanding electric mixer with dough hook, kneading for about 6 minutes. Place the dough in an oiled bowl and cover with a damp tea towel, leaving to rise for about 1 hour, or until doubled in size.

2 Preheat the oven to 230°C/Gas 8.

3 Melt the butter in a saucepan over a medium heat. Stir in the garlic and pesto, and take it off the heat.

4 Put the piece of baking paper on the worktop, dust with flour and put the risen dough on it. Roll it out, dusting your rolling pin with flour, until it is a rough rectangle the size of the paper. Slide the paper, dough rectangle still on it, on to the baking sheet.

5 Liberally paint about two-thirds of the garlic pesto butter all over the dough with the pastry brush, and leave to rest for about 25 minutes.

6 Bake for about 20 minutes, or until golden brown, the butter has soaked in, and the bread has bubbled up in places. Remove from the oven and paint with the remaining butter mix.

7 To make the balsamic syrup, simply place the balsamic vinegar and sugar in a small saucepan over a high heat. Allow to boil until it has reduced by half, then cool slightly before drizzling all over the baked bread.

8 Finish with a generous sprinkle of Parmesan cheese, strew the basil leaves on top, and season with pepper and sea salt flakes.

Essential equipment
Large baking sheet
   (32×46cm/13×18 inches)
A piece of baking paper
   cut to fit the baking sheet
Pastry brush

MEAT AND STUFFING PIE
SERVES 8–12

For the hot-water-crust pastry
250g plain flour
50g wholemeal flour
1 tsp salt
120ml water
100g lard
1 tbsp olive oil
A dash of Worcestershire sauce

For the stuffing
50g salted butter
Few drops olive oil
½ onion, very finely chopped
4 rashers smoked streaky
    bacon, finely chopped
4 sage leaves, finely chopped
100g white breadcrumbs
50g dried cranberries
Pinch of salt and pepper

For the filling
250g pork loin, diced
    into 5mm chunks
170g chicken breast,
    diced into 5mm chunks
½ onion, very finely chopped
½ tsp dried thyme
Pinch of salt and pepper

Being a lad from Wigan, I adore a good pie. I've even indulged in a 'Wigan kebab' once or twice – a pie inside a buttered barm cake – but I was very young and foolish, and probably intoxicated, so please forgive me. This is a delicious pie, and a creation I am very proud of. It is a hot-water-crust pastry, encasing delicious and succulent pork and chicken, with a cranberry and smoked bacon stuffing on top, finished with a sharp cider gelatine. Enough to make even the most pie-savvy Wiganer drool. I serve this with a big dollop of piccalilli.

1 Preheat the oven to 200°C/Gas 6.

2 To make the pastry, place the flours and salt in a heatproof bowl and stir together with a wooden spoon. Put the water, lard, oil and Worcestershire sauce in a saucepan over a high heat and bring to the boil. When the liquid is boiling ferociously and the lard is melted, remove from the heat and allow to cool for a minute, then pour it into the flour. Stir the contents of the bowl together with a wooden spoon until it all comes together in a thick, greasy pastry. When the liquids have become absorbed into the flour, it should be just cool enough to use your hands, so do so. Knead the pastry together on the worktop for a minute or so until it is smooth and doughy.

3 Split the pastry into two balls of two-thirds and one-third in size, and allow to cool for a few minutes.

4 Roll the two-thirds of pastry out on a well-floured work surface until about 3mm thick. Line the cake tin with this, ensuring it is well pressed into the corners.

There should be some overhang; just fold it over the edge of the tin, as you will trim it all later. Roll the one-third portion out so that it is slightly bigger than the diameter of the cake tin and place this on the baking sheet – this will form a lid for the pie. Place the lined tin and the pastry lid in the fridge until needed.

5 To make the stuffing, place the butter and oil in a frying pan and set over a high heat. Add the onion and bacon, and fry until the bacon is cooked and the onions are soft and translucent, about 5 minutes. Add the sage and fry for a few moments more, stirring the contents together. Remove the pan from the heat and add the breadcrumbs, cranberries, salt and pepper and mix together into a stiff stuffing. Set to one side.

6 To prepare the filling, put the pork and chicken in a bowl along with the onion, thyme, salt and pepper. Mix together well.

7 Remove the lined cake tin and lid from the fridge. Put the meat filling in the tin and press it down slightly. Place the stuffing on top so it covers the entire surface of the meat. Using a little of the beaten egg yolk, glaze the edges of the pastry where the lid will stick. Place the lid on top and crimp the pastry together using the thumb and forefinger of one hand, and the forefinger of the other. Make a hole of about 1cm in diameter in the lid.

8 Bake the pie for 40 minutes, then reduce the heat to 160°C/Gas 3 and bake for a further 30 minutes. Remove the pie from the cake tin and place on a

CONTINUED OVERLEAF

To finish
1 egg yolk, beaten with a tiny
    pinch of salt, for glazing
2 leaves of gelatine
300ml dry Suffolk cider
1 chicken stock cube

Essential equipment
20cm/8-inch shallow
    loose-bottomed cake tin
Baking sheet

baking sheet. Glaze the whole pie with the remaining beaten egg yolk, then pop back into the oven at 200°C/Gas 6 for 20 minutes more. All this may seem like a bit of a faff, but you want to ensure that the filling is cooked through without burning the pastry. If the pastry does start to go too dark, cover the pie with a sheet of foil.

9 Remove from the oven and allow to cool completely while you make the gelatine. Soak the gelatine leaves in cold water for 5 minutes to soften them. Pour the cider into a medium saucepan and allow to boil over a high heat for a minute or two to remove the bitter alcohol taste. Remove from the heat and stir in the stock cube. Drain the gelatine leaves and squeeze out any excess water, then add to the cider and stir until completely dissolved. Pour this into a heatproof jug.

10 Pour the jelly into the hole you made in the pastry lid. It will probably take a while to soak in and you will need to be patient with this. I find it helpful to have a piece of kitchen paper to hand, so that if liquid overflows you can soak it up before the pastry gets sodden. Once you have managed to get every last drop of liquid into the pie, place it in the fridge to set overnight.

PECAN AND CHOCOLATE PLAIT
SERVES 6–8

1 quantity Rough Puff Pastry
(see page 22) or 500g shop-
bought, all-butter puff pastry
Flour for dusting

For the pecan frangipane filling
170g salted butter,
at room temperature
100g light brown
muscovado sugar
70g caster sugar
3 eggs
120g pecan nuts, finely ground
50g cocoa powder

For the topping
75g chocolate chips
200g pecan nuts, bashed
1 egg, beaten with a tiny
pinch of salt, for glazing
1 tbsp icing sugar for dusting

Essential equipment
Baking sheet (at least
25×35cm/10×14 inches)
lined with baking paper
Piping bag with large
star nozzle

When I'm going through a greedy phase (which seems to happen a lot), I sneak into my local bakery and order a pecan plait. I devour it with a hot chocolate or mocha coffee and find myself in a state of complete, self-indulgent bliss. It is said that people should share, so I created a giant version of the plait with chocolate baked into it. Even though it is a huge pastry, I could probably still finish it off myself. Just don't tell anyone I told you.

1 Preheat the oven to 200°C/Gas 6.

2 Flour the worktop and roll the pastry out into a rectangle of 25x35cm. Place the pastry on the lined baking sheet, on which you will make the plait later. Set aside.

3 To make the frangipane filling, cream together the butter and both sugars until light and fluffy, then whisk in the eggs. Fold in the ground pecans and cocoa powder, and fill the piping bag with the mixture.

4 Place the pastry, on its baking sheet, in front of you, with one of the shorter edges facing you. Pipe one line of frangipane filling down the centre of the pastry, then a line either side of that, then a fourth and final line down the middle, on top of the first line. Leave about 10cm of uncovered pastry on either side of the filling. Sprinkle the chocolate chips and bashed pecans on top, and gently press them into it, avoiding spreading the filling out.

5 Take a sharp knife or pizza wheel and slice the pastry at either side of the filling into flaps 1cm wide, cutting away from the filling. So you should see before you a line of filling, with lots of little pastry flaps coming out of it. (Rather like a centipede, though a very tasty one.)

6 Glaze the edges of the flaps with some of the beaten egg, using a pastry brush or your finger. To make the plait, take the first flap from one side – the first being the flap furthest away from you – and fold it over the filling on a very slight diagonal. You may need to stretch the flap ever so slightly to get it over the filling. Press the flap gently into position so that it doesn't spring back, then do the same with the first flap on the other side, so that they meet. Repeat this until all the flaps of pastry are tightly plaited around the filling. The ends of the plait will be open and you will be able to see the filling, so do as I do – take a teaspoon and scrape a little of the filling out, then squeeze the ends of the pastry together to seal it. This ensures the filling doesn't leak out and make a right old mess during cooking.

7 Glaze the whole plait with the remaining egg, then bake for 30–35 minutes, or until the plait is puffed and golden. Remove from the oven and sift the icing sugar over the top. Serve hot or cold.

MOCHA CHOCA MADELEINES WITH CHOCOLATE DIPPING SAUCE MAKES 16

100g salted butter
2 eggs
100g caster sugar
1½ tsp instant freeze-
   dried coffee
85g plain flour
15g cocoa powder

For the sauce
2 tbsp golden syrup
2 tbsp cocoa powder
1 tbsp water

Essential equipment
16-hole madeleine tin
   (or a 12-hole shallow bun
   tin), greased and floured

Dipping these light, chocolaty, coffee cakes into a velvet chocolate sauce is a soothing, indulgent experience. If you don't have a 16-hole madeleine tin and you don't want to buy one, grease and flour a 12-hole bun tin and use that instead, baking for a few minutes longer.

1 Preheat the oven to 190°C/Gas 5.

2 Melt the butter in a saucepan over a medium heat. Do not let it boil. Set aside.

3 Put the eggs, sugar and coffee in a mixing bowl and beat with a hand-held electric whisk until light and fluffy and tripled in volume. If you have a freestanding electric mixer, you can do this using the whisk attachment. This will take 12–15 minutes.

4 Sift the flour and cocoa powder into the egg mixture, and pour in the butter. Gently, and I mean gently, fold these additions into the egg until smooth and silky.

5 Divide the mixture between the holes of the prepared madeleine mould – I find it works out at 2 teaspoons per madeleine (2½ using the bun tin). Bake for 8–10 minutes (a minute or two longer if using a bun tin), or until the madeleines look slightly browned around the edge. Turn them out of the tin as soon as they are baked or they will stick.

6 To make the sauce, simply whisk together the ingredients until you have a smooth, glossy dip.

GINGER NUT AND WHITE CHOCOLATE TART

SERVES 8–12

400g ginger nut biscuits
100g salted butter
400g white chocolate
400g double cream
2 eggs

Essential equipment
Food processor
25cm/10-inch loose-
  bottomed flan tin

I created this recipe to be gobbled up on Christmas Eve with strong coffee, but it would make a perfect indulgent treat at any time of the year.

1 Preheat the oven to 150°C/Gas 2.

2 Place the biscuits and butter in a food processor and blitz until you have a buttery, gingery sand. Pour this rubble into the flan tin and press down using the back of a spoon so that the buttery biscuit lines the base and sides of the tin. Place in the fridge.

3 Finely chop the chocolate and place in a large heatproof mixing bowl. Heat the cream in a saucepan over a high heat until bubbles just begin to appear at the edges. Remove from the heat, pour on to the chocolate and then, using a balloon whisk, mix together into a smooth ganache. Allow this to cool for a few minutes, then whisk in the eggs.

4 Pour the chocolate mixture into the biscuit-lined tin. Bake for 30–40 minutes, or until just set. Remove and allow to cool completely before serving.

TRILLIONAIRE'S SHORTBREAD

MAKES 12 OR 24

Who could resist? I don't think a biscuit could be any more indulgent. If you are in the mood for treating yourself, forget diets and get making a batch of these sinful soothers. The caramel in this isn't as solid as the shop-bought slices. This is indulgent, gooey and sticky. The ganache topping is deliciously creamy-firm.

For the shortbread
110g caster sugar
225g salted butter,
    at room temperature
Seeds from 1 vanilla pod,
    or 1 tsp vanilla paste
    or extract
340g plain flour

For the caramel
300g caster sugar
3 tbsp water
80g salted butter,
    in 1cm cubes
120ml double cream
1 tsp sea salt flakes

For the ganache
150g dark chocolate
150g milk chocolate
150ml double cream

Essential equipment
Deep-sided 20×25cm/
    8×10-inch baking tray,
    lined with baking paper

1 Preheat the oven to 180°C/Gas 4.

2 To make the shortbread, cream the sugar and butter together along with the vanilla. When light and fluffy, sift in the flour and mix into a firm dough. Press this into the base of the baking tray, prick all over with a fork, then refrigerate for 10 minutes. Bake for 15–20 minutes or until a pale golden colour. Allow to cool.

3 To make the caramel, stir the sugar and water together in a saucepan, then place over a high heat and allow to go a dark amber colour without stirring it again. When it goes amber, remove from the heat immediately and stir in the butter, cream and sea salt flakes (be careful as it will spit ferociously). Use a balloon whisk to beat together for a few minutes, or until smooth and light. Pour this on to the baked shortbread base and allow to firm up.

4 Make the ganache by chopping both chocolates and placing them in a heatproof bowl. Warm the cream in a saucepan over a high heat until bubbles just start to form around the edges. Pour the cream on to the chocolate, wait for 10 seconds, then, using a balloon whisk, beat until you have a smooth, glossy ganache. If there are still lumps of chocolate in the mix, you can either fish them out and eat them, or leave them in for added texture. Pour the ganache over the caramel, then cover the tray in foil, being careful not to touch the ganache, and refrigerate for at least 1 hour. When set, cut into 12 or 24 triangles.

INDIVIDUAL APPLE STRUDELS
MAKES 6

8 medium Granny
   Smith apples
150g caster sugar
150g dried sweetened
   cranberries
2 tbsp whisky
200g walnuts, chopped
200g marzipan, frozen
   30 minutes before use
12 sheets of filo pastry
125g unsalted butter,
   melted
Icing sugar to dust

Essential equipment
Pastry brush
Baking sheet, lined
   with baking paper

*When I visit the Manchester Christmas Markets –
probably twice a day all December – I treat myself to a
strudel soaked in custard. The soft apples and spices are
so heart-warming, and the strudel makes me feel merry
and festive. I wanted to create a version that could be
served as pudding at any time of year, and so I created
these gorgeous strudelettes filled with soft sweet apples,
cranberries, walnuts and marzipan (see overleaf).
I serve them with hot custard and cold ice cream.*

1 Preheat the oven to 200°C/Gas 6.

2 Peel and core the apples and dice them into 1cm
cubes. Place immediately in a mixing bowl with the
caster sugar, cranberries, whisky and walnuts and mix
together, so the apples don't get a chance to go brown.
Remove the marzipan from the freezer and grate into
bowl. Place to one side until needed.

3 Remove the filo pastry from its packet and unfold/
unroll it. Lay the piled sheets on the worktop and
cover them with a dampened tea towel; otherwise
they dry out.

4 Take one sheet of filo and paint it with melted butter,
then place another sheet neatly on top and paint that
with butter too. Spoon about a sixth of the filling on
to the filo in a fat sausage shape about 5cm from one
short edge, leaving about 2.5cm of pastry free at each
side. Gently pull the 5cm of filo over the filling, fold
the sides up, then roll the filling up in the pastry. It
should resemble an oversized spring roll. Place this
on the baking sheet, seam-side under, and repeat.
You should end up with 6 strudels.

5 Paint the strudels with the remaining butter and
sprinkle generously with icing sugar. Bake for 15
minutes, then reduce the heat to 180°C/Gas 4 and
bake for 20–25 minutes more. Allow to cool slightly
before sprinkling with more icing sugar and serving.

SPICED STICKY TOFFEE PUDDING
SERVES 8–12

100g dried pitted dates
100g dried figs
60g dried apricots
250ml apple and ginger
   tea (made from hot water
   and 1 tea bag)
100ml milk
60g salted butter, at room
   temperature
255g light brown
   muscovado sugar
2 eggs
Seeds from 1 vanilla pod,
   or 1 tsp vanilla paste
   or extract
1 tsp bicarbonate of soda
1 tsp mixed spice
310g self-raising flour

For the sauce
225g salted butter
310g dark brown
   muscovado sugar
200ml whipping cream

Essential equipment
Food processor (you can
   manage without one)
Glass or ceramic roasting
   dish of about 35×22cm/
   14×9 inches, greased

Even after a filling dinner, my friends are willing to loosen their belts and dig straight into this pudding. When I made it on stage for a food show, there were orders coming in from other stands and chefs, which speaks for itself. If you are in need of unadulterated indulgence, this is the pudding for you! I love this with ice cream, but I don't think it could be any better than with a good dollop of double cream.

1 Preheat the oven to 180°C/Gas 4.

2 Put the dried fruits in a food processor and blitz to a fruity mush. Add the tea and milk and blitz into a runny mass. Add the remaining ingredients for the pudding and blitz into a batter. Pour into the greased dish and bake for about 40 minutes or until baked through and spongy.

3 If you don't have a food processor, simply chop the fruits as finely as possible and soak them in the tea for 30 minutes. Then cream together the butter and sugar in a mixing bowl, using a wooden spoon. Stir in the remaining ingredients, including the tea-soaked fruits, and continue as above.

4 When baked, remove from the oven and allow to cool completely.

5 To make the sauce, put the butter, sugar and cream in a saucepan over a medium heat and allow to melt. Bring to the boil, stirring constantly, then pour the sauce over the cooled pudding, still in its dish. Return the whole thing to the oven and bake for a further 35 minutes. Serve at once.

CHERRY BRANDY AND BRAZIL NUT BROWNIES

MAKES 16

100g dark chocolate
80g milk chocolate
125g salted butter
2 eggs
3 tbsp mayonnaise
125g light brown
   muscovado sugar
85g caster sugar
70ml cherry brandy
Seeds from 2 vanilla pods,
   or 2 tsp vanilla paste
   or extract
180g plain flour
3 tbsp cocoa powder
100g Brazil nuts, roughly
   chopped

Essential equipment
23cm/9-inch square loose-
   bottomed cake tin, greased
   and lined with baking paper

There is a lot of debate circling around the humble brownie: flour or no flour; soggy or cake-like? For me, if it's chocolaty and slightly gooey, it's a brownie. These in particular are delicious – the cherry brandy leaves a fruity aftertaste, while the Brazil nuts give a perfect crunch. Mayonnaise may seem like a strange addition, but I beg you to try it. It doesn't impart any taste to the brownies; what it does is allow them to stay gooey.

1 Preheat the oven to 180°C/Gas 4.

2 Finely chop both chocolates, place in a heatproof mixing bowl set over a pan of simmering water and allow to melt. Dice the butter and stir into the melted chocolate until glossy. Remove from the heat and allow to cool for a minute.

3 Beat in the eggs and mayonnaise. I find it satisfying to do this with a wooden spoon, but you could transfer it all to a freestanding electric mixer if you wish.

4 Beat in the remaining ingredients until you have a smooth, velvety batter with chunks of nuts. Pour into the prepared tin and bake for 20–25 minutes, or until the top is cracked but the underneath still slightly soft. Allow to cool completely in the tin before slicing into chunks or wedges.

VARIATIONS

To make chocolate and chilli brownies, omit the Brazil nuts, swap the cherry brandy for sherry or milk, and add to the flour 1 finely chopped red chilli.

To make double chocolate brownies, replace the cherry brandy with 70ml milk, and replace the Brazil nuts with 50g each of milk and white chocolate chips.

CHOCOLATE AND CASSIS CAKE SERVES 8–12

85g dark chocolate,
   roughly chopped
170g salted butter,
   at room temperature
225g light brown
   muscovado sugar
60ml sunflower oil
200g self-raising flour
25g cocoa powder
4 eggs
½ tsp Worcestershire Sauce

For the drizzle syrup
50g caster sugar
50ml water
50ml crème de cassis liqueur

For the filling
300ml double cream
4 tbsp crème de cassis liqueur
200g blackcurrants (or
   blackberries if currants
   are difficult to find)

Essential equipment
2×20cm/8-inch loose-
   bottomed round sandwich
   tins, greased and lined
   with baking paper

This is certainly something to desire. While I adore chocolate cake, I think it needs a certain something to soften the potential bitterness. Here, the cassis and blackcurrants complement the chocolate very well. A potentially shocking savoury ingredient is the Worcestershire sauce. I find that chocolate really does get a boost when mixed with a savoury shot. The Aztecs used chilli; I use my faithful store-cupboard stalwart.

1 Preheat the oven to 150°C/Gas 2.

2 Place the chocolate in a heatproof bowl set over a pan of barely simmering water. Allow to melt, then remove from the heat and set to one side.

3 To make the cake, beat the butter and sugar together in a large mixing bowl – or the bowl of a freestanding electric mixer – until paler in colour and lighter in texture. Add the oil and mix in well. Add the melted, cooled chocolate and beat that in, then add the rest of the ingredients and mix to a smooth batter.

4 Divide between the cake tins. Bake for 25–30 minutes, on the same shelf if possible, until a skewer inserted into the centre of each cake comes out clean. Allow to cool for 5 minutes, then remove the cakes from their tins and allow to cool completely.

5 For the drizzle syrup, put the sugar and water in a small saucepan, bring to the boil, then reduce slightly for 3 minutes. Remove from the heat and stir in the crème de cassis.

6 Place one cake on a cake stand and drizzle half the syrup over it. Drizzle the rest over the other cake.

7 To make the filling, whip the cream to soft, floppy peaks and fold in the liqueur and blackcurrants. Pile the cream on top of the first cake, then place the second cake on top. Best eaten on the day of making.

VARIATION
For a beautiful 3-layer cake, divide the cake mixture between 3 sandwich tins, and use double the amount of filling.

CHOCOLATE ORANGE TARTLETS
MAKES 12

1 quantity Rich Sweet
  Shortcrust Pastry
  (see page 21)
200g milk chocolate,
  finely chopped
100ml single cream
Zest 1 small orange
2 tbsp Cointreau liqueur

Essential equipment
7.5cm/3-inch round
  cookie cutter
12-hole shallow bun tin
Baking paper and beans
  or rice

Indulgence can't be more easily found than in the combination of chocolate and orange. These sweet treats are so easy to make that really it's more assembling than baking. But I won't tell if you don't.

1 Make the pastry according to the recipe on page 21, then allow to rest in the fridge for 30 minutes.

2 Preheat the oven to 180°C/Gas 4.

3 Roll out the pastry to about 4mm thick, and cut out 12 circles using the cookie cutter. Use these to line the bun tin, pricking the base of each one with a fork. Cut out 12 squares of baking paper, larger than the holes of the tin, and line the pastry with these. Fill each square with baking beans or dried rice, and bake for 12 minutes. Take out of the oven, remove the paper and beans, then return the cases to the oven to bake for a further 5 minutes. Allow to cool completely.

4 Make the filling by placing the chocolate in a heatproof bowl. Heat the cream in a small saucepan over a medium heat, until it is just hot enough that you can't hold your finger in it. Stir in most of the orange zest – keep some for decoration – and the Cointreau, then pour this over the chocolate. Stir until the chocolate has melted and you have a glossy ganache. If the chocolate doesn't completely melt, fill the saucepan with hot water from the tap and place back on the medium heat. Set the bowl over this saucepan and stir constantly until thick and glossy.

5 Fill each pastry shell to the brim with chocolate ganache, then top with a sprinkle of orange zest.

DARK CHOCOLATE AND GINGER COOKIES

MAKES 32

180g salted butter,
  at room temperature
200g light brown
  muscovado sugar
100g stem ginger balls
  in syrup, drained and
  finely chopped
1 egg
250g plain flour
1 tsp baking powder
150g dark chocolate chips

Essential equipment
4 baking sheets lined with
  baking paper (2 if you
  are making 16 cookies)

I have loved dark chocolate and ginger ever since I was a very small boy. My family used to think I was bizarre as I tucked into a bag of dark-chocolate-coated stem ginger. Most kids would barf into their hankies at the smell of it, but I – a prodigy, I like to think – loved the bitterness and heat. These are a complete indulgence and one that I believe is best unshared and selfishly devoured. Having said that, even I struggle to eat 32 cookies. I recommend using half the mixture to make 16, rolling the rest of the dough into a long sausage, wrapping it in cling film and freezing until the next desire for ginger cookies overtakes you . . .

1 Preheat the oven to 160°C/Gas 3.

2 Place the butter and sugar in a mixing bowl and beat until well mixed, pale and fluffy – you could do this in a freestanding electric mixer with paddle attachment, or using a hand-held electric mixer.

3 Add the stem ginger and egg and beat until well incorporated. Finally, add the flour, baking powder and chocolate chips, and mix together to form a firm cookie dough. Chill the dough in the fridge for at least 30 minutes. This makes it easier to work with.

4 Carve out heaped teaspoonfuls of the dough and roll them in your palms into little balls. Place spaced well apart on the baking sheets – I get about 8 balls on each sheet, so do this in batches. Bake for 15–20 minutes, or until lightly golden in colour and a little darker round the edges. Allow to cool completely before devouring unashamedly.

CHAPTER NINE
THE ARTIST WITHIN

I've never been particularly artistic, not in the orthodox 'paintbrush and paint' sense at any rate. It's like I have two left hands. To top it all off I am colour blind, so there really is no hope for me. Hockney can sleep soundly at night, knowing there is no competition coming from this direction.

Having said that, I do have some artistic yearning burning away inside me and baking is my expression of that, so you could say that the recipes in this chapter come from the artist in me. That's not to say that these recipes are works of art – that's not it at all. Rather, some are perhaps a little trickier than others and so I tackle them when feeling confident. Others offer inspiring flavour combinations.

CURRIED HALLOUMI, SPINACH AND POTATO PITHIVIER
SERVES 8

2 tbsp olive oil
Knob of salted butter
1 tsp cumin powder
1 tsp ground coriander
1 tsp yellow mustard seeds
1 tsp chilli powder
1 tsp turmeric
½ tsp garam masala
¼ tsp ground ginger
¼ tsp smoked paprika
3 cloves
Pinch of nutmeg
2 onions, very finely chopped
2 garlic cloves, minced
2 tsp cider vinegar
2 tsp dark brown sugar
1 tbsp tomato purée
200g spinach leaves
1 tsp chicken stock concentrate
Salt and pepper
Small handful of fresh
  coriander, chopped
450g halloumi (Cypriot cheese)
7 new potatoes
1 quantity Rough Puff Pastry
  (see page 22) or 500g shop-
  bought all-butter puff
1 egg, beaten with a tiny
  pinch of salt, for glazing

Essential equipment
Large baking sheet, lined
  with baking paper

I love to mix things up a little and cross cultures in one dish. That is what I've done here: you have the traditional notion of a French pithivier, filled with a gloriously spiced halloumi, spinach and potato curry inspired by the Indian subcontinent. When you are feeling creative, trying something new like this is fun, and the taste is so rewarding. The ingredients list might look long, but many of these ingredients will be in your store cupboard, and, if not, they really aren't expensive.

1 Put the oil and butter in a large saucepan and heat on medium-high until the butter has melted into the oil. Add the ingredients starting with the cumin down to the nutmeg, and allow to warm and infuse the oil for a minute or so.

2 Then add the onions, garlic, vinegar and sugar and turn up the heat. Fry for about 2 minutes, or until the onions are just softening.

3 Add the purée, spinach, chicken stock concentrate, salt, pepper and chopped coriander, and reduce the heat to low. Allow the spinach to wilt into the sauce, before removing the pan from the heat and allowing it to cool completely.

4 Cut the halloumi into 1cm cubes and set aside.

5 Slice the new potatoes into 5mm-thick discs. Bring a large pan of water to the boil, add a generous pinch of salt, add the potato slices and boil for 12 minutes.

CONTINUED OVERLEAF

CURRIED HALLOUMI, SPINACH AND POTATO PITHIVIER
CONTINUED

6 Drain the potatoes and allow to cool completely.

7 Preheat the oven to 180°C/Gas 4.

8 Roll the pastry to about 3mm thick and cut out 2 large discs measuring 25cm across. You may need to cut out one disc, then stack up the trimmings and re-roll in order to get the second. Place one of the discs on the baking sheet and place the cooled potatoes on it, overlapping them in concentric circles and leaving a 1cm clear perimeter around the edge.

9 Mix the halloumi into the curry sauce, taste and season if necessary, then pile this on top of the potatoes, remembering to leave the 1cm perimeter completely clear. Using a little of the beaten egg, glaze the perimeter of the bottom disc. Place the second disc of pastry on top of the curry mound, and press the edges of the discs together all the way round. Crimp the discs together, or use a fork to make a pattern and seal the discs together.

10 Glaze the pithivier with egg wash – but not the thin crust as that might make it burn. With the back of a knife blade, score a sunburst pattern on top. Bake in the preheated oven. After 10 minutes, turn the oven up to 200°C/Gas 6, and bake for a further 20–25 minutes.

'WHICH CAME FIRST' PIE

SERVES 6–8

5 tbsp olive oil

2 large onions, roughly chopped

2 garlic cloves, finely chopped

Salt and pepper

100ml white wine

800g boneless and skinless chicken thigh meat, diced

2 heaped tbsp plain flour

½ tsp mustard powder

1 chicken stock cube in 300ml freshly boiled water (or 300ml fresh chicken stock)

150g chestnut mushrooms, sliced

200ml double cream

Leaves from 5 sprigs of thyme

Small handful parsley, finely chopped

8 hard-boiled eggs

1 quantity Rough Puff Pastry (see page 22) or 500g shop-bought all-butter puff

Essential equipment

Pie dish, about 35×20cm/ 14×8 inches

The question of whether the chicken or the egg came first has plagued people for years, and is sure to do so for years to come, but I am simply grateful there are eggs and chickens to stuff into this tasty pie. Regardless of which came first, they both end up in the same pot, with mushrooms, white wine, thyme and cream, and … what was the question again?

1 Put 3 tablespoons of the oil in a large saucepan over a high heat. Add the onions and garlic, turn the heat down to medium-low, add a good pinch of salt and the wine, and allow the onions to cook down for about 15 minutes, or until translucent and sloppy. Remove from the pan and place in a bowl for later.

2 Turn the heat back up, put in the rest of the oil, add the diced chicken meat and cook until browned all over, removing it from the pan when done. You may need to do this in batches so you don't overcrowd the pan (which brings the temperature down).

3 When all the meat is browned, return it to the pan, along with the onions. Turn the heat down to medium, sift the flour and mustard powder over the contents of the pan, stir well, and cook off the floury taste for a minute or two. Now add the stock, mushrooms, cream, half a teaspoon each of salt and pepper, and the thyme and parsley. Allow this to heat for about 5 minutes, stirring often. If after this time you think the gravy isn't thick enough, add another tablespoon of flour and mix in well.

4 Preheat the oven to 220°C/Gas 7.

5 Place the eggs in the pie dish, then ladle in the pie filling, being careful not to displace the eggs. Allow this to cool. Roll out the pastry to just larger than the size of the pie dish. Wet the edges of the dish, and place the pastry on top. Slash some steam holes in the centre. Bake for about 40 minutes, or until the pastry is nicely golden and the filling is bubbling through the steam holes.

BAKLAVA MILLEFEUILLE
MAKES 8

1 quantity Crème Pâtissière
  (see page 24)
A few drops of rosewater,
  to taste (optional)
100g apricots
100g unsalted
  pistachio kernels
6 sheets shop-bought
  filo pastry
75g unsalted butter, melted
Icing sugar, for dusting

Essential equipment
2 baking sheets
Pastry brush
Piping bag with large
  star nozzle

I love baklava, with its wonderful mix of chewy, fragrant filling and buttery filo pastry. This recipe, however, arose from sheer laziness. I had a packet of shop-bought filo pastry in the fridge. I was craving millefeuille, and so I thought I would cheat a bit and make it using the filo. As I was constructing the 'thousand layers', I had an idea to mix apricots and pistachios into the layers of pastry. A short while later, these delicious treats were born.

1 Make the crème pâtissière according to the recipe on page 24. When cooled, mix with the rosewater, if using, being careful not to use too much or you will end up with something too fragrant even for a Turkish bath. Set aside.

2 Grind together the apricots and pistachios in a food processor to a sticky mass. If you don't have a food processor, chop them together as finely as possible.

3 Preheat the oven to 190°C/Gas 5.

4 Place one piece of filo pastry on one of the baking sheets (it will probably be too long to fit, but don't worry). Keep the other sheets of filo under a damp tea towel to stop them drying out. Paint the pastry with melted butter, then sprinkle over some icing sugar. Fold the filo sheet in half lengthways, then paint the surface with more butter and dust with more icing sugar.

5 Place another piece of filo on top of this, paint with butter and dust with icing sugar, and then, before folding, spread half the apricot-pistachio mix all over it. Fold in half lengthways and lightly press so the filling flattens. Paint with butter and dust with sugar, then add the third and final sheet of filo, painting with butter and dusting with sugar, before folding in half.

6 Repeat this process with the 3 remaining filo sheets and the apricot-pistachio mix on the second baking sheet, before placing both sheets in the oven and baking for 15 minutes. (Swap them around after 7 minutes if they are on different shelves.)

7 When the pastry layers are baked, remove from the oven and immediately slice each one in half. Then slice at right angles to the first slice, so you have 4 quarters on each baking sheet. Slice these in half lengthways, so you have 8 long strips of layered filo on each baking sheet. Allow to cool.

8 When the pastry layers have cooled, put the crème pâtissière into the piping bag and pipe a tight zigzag down the length of 8 of the pastry layers. Top with the remaining pastry layers, and finish with a final flutter of icing sugar.

SALTED CARAMEL RUM BABAS

MAKES 4

225g plain flour
½ tsp salt
40g golden caster sugar
7g fast-action yeast (1 sachet)
4 eggs
2 tbsp milk
120g salted butter,
   at room temperature
   and cut into 1cm cubes

For the syrup
200g golden caster sugar
100ml water
2–3 tbsp toffee vodka (optional)

For the salted caramel drizzle
100g caster sugar
1 tbsp water
50ml double cream
30g salted butter
Pinch of sea salt flakes
Double cream, to serve

Essential equipment
4 × mini savarin/baba moulds
Butter and caster sugar
   for the moulds
Piping bag with a 2cm nozzle
2 large roasting tins

On the first episode of The Great British Bake-off, I made the near fatal error of using salt instead of sugar in my rum babas. On the bright side, though, it did make Paul Hollywood gag, which was hilarious to watch. I thought I would pay homage to that hilarity, and so, Paul, these are dedicated to you. With respect, gratitude and admiration.

1 To make the baba batter, place the flour in a mixing bowl and stir in the salt and sugar. Then stir the yeast through the flour too. Place the eggs and milk in a jug and beat together. Pour this into the dry ingredients. Using a wooden spoon or hand-held mixer, beat together for about 5 minutes. You could do this in a freestanding electric mixer with paddle attachment.

2 After about 5 minutes, add the butter in cubes, and beat well to incorporate into the mixture until it is smooth, elastic and satiny – about 5 more minutes. Cover the bowl with a damp tea towel and allow to rise for 1 hour.

3 Meanwhile, grease the moulds with butter. Place in the freezer for 10 minutes, then grease again and return to the freezer. In the final 5 minutes of the batter's proving time, remove the moulds from the freezer and sprinkle each one liberally with caster sugar, ensuring you cover all the inside. This will help to prevent the babas sticking.

CONTINUED OVERLEAF

SALTED CARAMEL RUM BABAS CONTINUED

4 After the batter has proved for a full hour, beat it a little with a wooden spoon, and then use it to fill the piping bag. Pipe the batter into the prepared moulds, creating a ring around the edge. This can be tricky, but try to ensure you divide it equally between the moulds, then wipe off any batter that has dripped on to the centre. Leave these to prove for another hour.

5 Preheat the oven to 180°C/Gas 4.

6 After the babas have proved for the second full hour, bake them for 20–25 minutes, or until golden brown and well risen.

7 Meanwhile, make the syrup by heating together the sugar and water in a medium saucepan over a high heat until boiling. Reduce the heat to low, heat gently for 2 minutes, then add the toffee vodka, if using. Remove the pan from the heat.

8 When the babas are baked, remove them immediately from their moulds. Pour one-third of the syrup into the baba moulds, then pop the babas back into the moulds to start soaking it up. Pour the remaining syrup into the roasting dishes, then place 2 babas in each, upside down, to soak up the syrup on their other side. Allow to soak for 5–10 minutes.

9 Make the salted caramel drizzle by stirring the sugar and water together in a medium saucepan, then placing the mixture over a high heat. Do not stir again: let the heat do the work. Boil for about 5 minutes or until the bubbles begin to reduce in size and the mixture turns amber. As soon as it does, add the cream and butter and mix well for a few seconds to create a smooth caramel – this will sputter, so do take care. Remove from the heat and mix in the salt.

10 Turn the babas out on to plates and drizzle with the salted caramel. Serve with a generous helping of double cream.

PECAN AND MAPLE BAGELS

MAKES 12

There is something really impressive about a home-made bagel. They aren't the easiest of breads to master, but nor are they impossibly difficult. Perfect at any time of the day, but particularly at elevenses.

For the dough
500g strong white flour
10g salt
7g fast-action yeast (1 sachet)
100g roughly chopped pecans
270ml tepid water
1 egg
2 tbsp maple syrup
1 tbsp olive oil
1 egg, beaten with a tiny
    pinch of salt, for glazing

For the maple glaze
50g pecan halves,
    roughly chopped
5 tbsp maple syrup
5 tbsp caster sugar

Essential equipment
2 baking sheets, dusted
    with flour

1 To make the dough, put the flour, salt, yeast and pecans in a mixing bowl. Put the water, egg, syrup and oil into a jug and whisk together. Slowly pour the liquid into the dry ingredients, mixing well with a fork. When the dough becomes too stiff to stir with a fork, use your hands to squeeze the dough together, then turn it out on to the worktop and knead for 10 minutes or until the dough is smooth and elastic.

2 Divide the dough into 12 (if you like to be exact, weigh out 12 pieces at 69g each), then roll into balls. Place each one well apart on the baking sheets, cover with a damp cloth and leave to rise for 30 minutes.

3 After 30 minutes, use the floured handle of a wooden spoon to make a hole in the centre of each ball. Stretch this hole out using your fingers, ensuring you get the sides of the bagels as neat and even as possible. Place back on the baking sheets, cover, and allow to rise for another 30 minutes.

4 After about 20 minutes, bring a large saucepan of water to the boil and preheat the oven to 210°C/Gas 7.

5 When the 30 minutes are up, drop the bagels in the boiling water 3 or 4 at a time, and boil on each side for 1 minute. Remove by fishing them out with a slotted spoon, holding them in place with the handle of a wooden spoon – they are extremely slippery – then drain on a cooling rack.

6 When dry, glaze each one with beaten egg and place back on the baking sheets, well spaced. Bake for 20–25 minutes, or until perfectly bronzed.

7 Boil the maple glaze ingredients until thick and syrupy. As soon as the bagels come out of the oven, place on the cooling rack and drench them in the glaze, using it all up.

LIME (BASIL) AND MANDARIN CHEESECAKE
SERVES 12–16

For the base
300g digestive biscuits
125g unsalted butter,
  cut into 1cm cubes

For the cheesecake filling
900g full-fat cream cheese,
  best quality possible
Seeds from 1 vanilla pod,
  or 1 tsp vanilla paste
  or extract
3 eggs
Zest of 2 limes
2 tbsp plain flour
50ml double cream
200g caster sugar

For the mandarin jelly
2 leaves of gelatine
300g can of mandarin
  segments in orange juice
Basil leaves to decorate

Essential equipment
23cm/9-inch springform
  cake tin, greased
Aluminium foil
Deep roasting tray

My favourite cologne is Lime, Basil and Mandarin by Jo Malone, and I wanted to create something that celebrated that gorgeous scent. The basil aspect of this dish is merely decoration, but it does add to the flavour nonetheless. This is a simple baked cheesecake with added lime zest, finished with a mandarin jelly and decorated with a few basil leaves. Because of the mandarin jelly topping, it is best left to set overnight.

1 Wrap the outside of the springform tin in foil. This will prevent any water leaking in and ruining the cheesecake when you bake it in a water bath. Preheat the oven to 200°C/Gas 6.

2 To make the base, place the biscuits and butter cubes in a food processor and blitz until the mixture resembles sand. Tip into the prepared tin and squash down so you have an even base. Bake for 15 minutes, then remove and allow to cool.

3 If you don't have a food processor, bash the biscuits into crumbs in a food bag, then pour them into a mixing bowl. Melt the butter over a medium temperature in a saucepan, and then pour it over the biscuit crumbs. Mix together well, tip into the tin and squash down. You will need to chill this in the fridge for 20 minutes before baking.

4 To make the cheesecake filling, put the cream cheese in a bowl and beat it with a wooden spoon until smooth. Add the vanilla, eggs and lime zest and mix well. Finally add the flour, cream and sugar, and stir together until incorporated.

CONTINUED OVERLEAF

LIME (BASIL) AND MANDARIN CHEESECAKE
CONTINUED

5 Now set the oven to 170°C/Gas 3. When the base has cooled a little, pour the filling over it. Place the whole tin – make sure the foil hasn't come loose – in a large roasting tray and into the oven. Pour boiling water into the roasting tray – ensure you don't get any in the cheesecake – to halfway up the side of the cake tin. Close the oven door and bake for 35–40 minutes or until set with a very slight wobble in the centre. Remove from the oven and allow to cool.

6 While the cheesecake is cooling, make the mandarin jelly top. Submerge the gelatine leaves in a bowl of cold water. Set to one side.

7 Pour the whole can of mandarins – juice and all – into a food processor and blitz until the segments are liquidized. Sieve into a pan, ensuring you get every last bit of juice. Discard the pulp in the sieve. Again, if you don't have a processor, pour the contents of the can into a sieve and squeeze out all the juice using the back of a spoon.

8 Heat the mandarin juice over a medium heat until just hot enough that you can't hold your finger in it. Drain the gelatine leaves, squeeze out the excess water and place in the pan of warm mandarin juice. Stir well until the leaves are dissolved, then allow to cool for 10 minutes before pouring over the top of the cheesecake. Place in the fridge and allow to set overnight.

9 Finish with a few basil leaves.

BREAD AND BUTTER CHRISTMAS PUD-PUD
SERVES 8–12

12 slices thick white bread,
  best if left overnight to stale
100g unsalted butter,
  at room temperature
500g leftover cooked
  Christmas pudding
150g light brown
  muscovado sugar, plus
  extra for sprinkling
500ml full-cream milk
  (or whole milk if that's
  the best you can get)
3 eggs

Essential equipment
Large roasting dish or large
  shallow Pyrex pudding tray
  – not a pudding basin

Christmas pudding is a fab festive treat that nonetheless seems to haunt my cupboards all year round. No matter how much pudding I use at Christmas, there always seem to be at least two shop-bought puds still nestled in a corner the following year. No longer am I haunted by these Christmas ghosts. With this recipe, a pudding is for life, not just for Christmas. This is perfect for after a Sunday dinner, served with both cream and sloppy vanilla ice cream – although I could eat it at any time, any day.

1 Preheat the oven to 200°C/Gas 6.

2 Butter the slices of bread. You can remove the crusts if you like, but I prefer them on. (If you do remove them, add another crustless slice.) Chop the slices into 2.5cm chunks and throw them into a large mixing bowl.

3 Crumble the pudding and add to the bread along with the sugar. Mix with your hands so the bread and pudding is evenly dispersed. Pile this mess into the roasting dish or pudding tray.

4 Make the custard by whisking together the milk and eggs. Pour this over the pudding and bread in stages, allowing it to soak in. When it's all in, set aside to soak up the custard for 10 more minutes, then sprinkle 1–2 tablespoons of light brown muscovado on top. Bake the pud-pud for 30–35 minutes, or until golden on top. Serve warm.

ALMOND AND PEAR CROWN TORTE

SERVES 6

For the pears
6 small conference pears
800ml water
400g caster sugar
1 cinnamon stick
1 vanilla pod, split in
    half lengthways
Zest of 1 lemon

For the torte
6 eggs, separated
300g ground almonds
2 tsp baking powder
2 tsp almond extract
200g golden caster sugar
Zest of 1 lemon

To finish
1 tbsp Demerara sugar
250g icing sugar
1 tbsp lemon juice

Essential equipment
23cm/9-inch springform
    cake tin, greased and lined

My brother-in-law, Mike, cannot eat food containing gluten, and being from a greedy family he naturally finds this difficult. I felt so sorry for him that I devised this grand, gluten-free torte just for him. It's perfect for a dinner party or other special occasion.

1 Peel the pears, but don't bother to core them, and leave the stalks on. Put the water in the saucepan and bring to a gentle boil. Add the sugar and stir to dissolve. Break the cinnamon stick into 4 pieces and add with the vanilla and zest. Turn the heat down to a gentle simmer and add the pears. Poach for 10–20 minutes, or until a knife can easily pierce the flesh but the pears retain their shape. Remove the pears and place on a sheet of kitchen paper to dry a little.

2 Meanwhile, preheat the oven to 150°C/Gas 2. To make the torte batter, place the egg whites in one mixing bowl and the egg yolks in another. To the bowl with the egg yolks, add the ground almonds, baking powder, almond extract, sugar and lemon zest, and mix together. This will be a very stiff mixture and so will take some elbow grease and a firm wooden spoon.

3 Using a hand-held electric mixer, or a freestanding mixer with whisk attachment, whisk the egg whites until they form stiff white peaks. Take a third of this egg white and beat it into the stiff egg yolk mixture to slacken it slightly. Then tip the rest of the egg white into the yolk mix, and fold in gently using a thin spatula. It will take a while to incorporate the egg whites so they are evenly distributed, but do try not to beat out too much air.

CONTINUED OVERLEAF

4 When the mix is even in colour and consistency, pour it gently into the tin. To avoid bursting any bubbles, don't pour it from a great height; get as close to the base of the tin as possible. Even off the batter with a spoon, then slot the pears around the edge, bottoms into the batter and stalky tops poking out. Sprinkle the top with Demerara sugar.

5 Bake for about 40–50 minutes or until the top feels set. Due to the oil content of the ground almonds, this might look uncooked until it sets fully, so don't be concerned if after this time it seems unbaked; I promise you it will be.

6 Remove from the oven but leave in the tin to cool completely. Mix together the lemon juice and icing sugar until the icing is pourable but thick – you may need to loosen it with a drop of water. Pour over the top of the cooled cake, and serve.

LITTLE SALTED CARAMEL GALETTES DES ROIS

MAKES 12–16

1 quantity Rough Puff Pastry
(see page 22) or 500g shop-
bought all-butter puff pastry

For the salted caramel
100g caster sugar
3 tbsp water
30g salted butter
30ml cream
1–2 tsp sea salt flakes

For the icing
2 tbsp water
250g icing sugar

Equipment
7.5cm/3-inch fluted
cookie cutter
1 or 2 baking sheets

In France the twelfth day of Christmas is usually celebrated with a galette des rois, a puff pastry round topped with sweet icing and sometimes filled with an almond paste or frangipane. My versions are individual sizes, and perfect as a little sweet treat with a nice cuppa in the afternoon.

1 Preheat the oven to 200°C/Gas 6.

2 Roll the pastry out to about 3mm thick, then cut out as many circles as you can from it using the cookie cutter. Spread these out on a baking sheet or two and bake for 20–25 minutes, or until beautifully puffed up and lightly golden.

3 While the pastry is baking, make the salted caramel by mixing the sugar and water in a medium saucepan. Place this over a high heat and allow to bubble away without stirring it any further (otherwise it will crystallize). When the sugar becomes a dark golden colour, add the butter and cream – this will sputter vigorously, so be careful not to burn yourself. Remove from the heat, add the salt, to taste, and mix with a wooden spoon. Set to one side for later.

4 When the pastry puffs are done, remove from the oven and allow to cool completely on a cooling rack set over a sheet of baking paper or foil (to catch drips). Make the icing by adding the water to the icing sugar a drop at a time – the icing needs to be pourable, but very thick. Pour the icing over the pastry puffs and allow it to spread. Finish with a good drizzle of the salted caramel.

LEMON MACARONS

For the macaron batter
130g ground almonds
170g icing sugar
3 egg whites
75g caster sugar
Yellow food colouring
  (pastes/gels are best)

For the buttercream
80g unsalted butter,
  at room temperature
230g icing sugar
2 tbsp freshly squeezed
  lemon juice
Zest of 2 lemons

Essential equipment
2 baking sheets lined
  with baking paper
Food processor
Piping bags with 1cm
  and 2cm plain nozzles

Macarons have a reputation of being tricky to make, and I have to admit they are not the easiest to get exactly right, but I don't think that should be a reason not to have a good go. Lemon macarons are quite my most favourite of all, because the bitter lemon cuts perfectly through the sweetness, and those two elements together in a crisp but chewy treat is sheer heaven.

1 Using a 10p coin as a guide, cover each piece of paper on the baking sheets with circles, ensuring you leave a good inch between each one. You need about 25 circles on each sheet of baking paper. Set these aside for later.

2 To make the macaron batter, place the almonds and icing sugar in a food processor and blitz so the mixture is as fine as possible. (I highly recommend using a food processor for this.) When you have blitzed the mixture, sieve it into a large mixing bowl and place to one side.

3 Place the egg whites in a large, preferably metal, mixing bowl and, using a hand-held electric mixer, whisk them until they start to foam up. Continue beating until the egg whites hold peaks that are neither too soft nor too stiff.

4 Continue beating slowly as you add the caster sugar a tablespoon at a time – when you have added half the caster sugar, stop beating, put some yellow food colouring gel on the end of your electric mixer blade, then continue mixing and adding sugar. If the colour isn't quite lemon yellow, add a little more colouring.

CONTINUED OVERLEAF

5 Once you've added all the sugar, whisk for a final 30 seconds, then stop beating. With a rubber spatula, gently scrape the coloured meringue on top of the almond powder mix.

6 Now this is the most fundamental stage of macaron making – mixing the ingredients together. The French call it 'macaronage'. Using a narrow rubber spatula or metal spoon or even a narrow plastic dough scraper, fold the almond powder mix and egg whites together by scraping around the side of the bowl then cutting through the centre of the mix, and repeating this motion, ensuring you incorporate the ingredients from the bottom of the bowl, until you have a smooth batter, which drops from your mixing implement in a thick, magma-like way. If the batter is too thick, air pockets will get trapped and cause the macaron shells to crack. Too thin, and the macarons will spread out and be unusable.

7 Carefully and gently fill a piping bag fitted with a 1cm nozzle with the macaron mixture. Twist the end of the piping bag together, then, holding the bag upright, pipe blobs of batter on to the baking paper, just filling the 10p-piece-sized circles you drew.

8 Once you have piped the blobs of batter, gently pick up the baking sheets and bang them on the worktop 3 or 4 times to expel any large air bubbles. If any of the macaron blobs have peaks of batter sticking up, gently flatten them with a dampened finger. Leave for at least 1 hour in a draught-free place so the shells can form a shiny coating.

9 Preheat the oven to 170°C/Gas 3.

10 Make the buttercream by blitzing the butter and icing sugar in a food processor until well mixed. Add the lemon juice and zest and blitz again. Keep in a cool place until needed.

11 Once the macaron shells have rested for 1 hour, slide one of the baking sheets into the oven and bake for 12 minutes, during which time, at 4-minute intervals, you need to open the oven door rapidly then close it immediately. This releases over-hot air, and humidity. So you bake the shells for 4 minutes, open and close the door, bake for another 4 minutes, open and close the door, then bake for a final 4 minutes before removing the shells from the oven. Bake the second sheet of macaron shells in the same way.

12 Allow the baked shells to cool completely before removing from the baking paper. Someone once told me to imagine you are peeling the baking paper from the macaron shells, and not the other way round, and I find this helps to keep the shells from breaking.

13 Finally fill a piping bag fitted with a 2cm plain nozzle with the buttercream and pipe a blob of this on to half of the shells. Sandwich these shells together with the other shells. Wasn't so tricky, was it?

RICH CHICK MACARONS

Follow the recipe above, replacing 30g of the almonds with cocoa powder, and omitting the food colouring. For the filling, place a blob of strawberry jam in the centre of half of the macaron shells. Make the buttercream recipe in the same way, but substitute a sweet wine or champagne for the lemon juice. Pipe this champagne buttercream around the blob of jam, then place the other half shells on top. Decorate, if you wish, with gold leaf.

CROQUEMBOUCHE
SERVES 12

1 quantity Crème Pâtissière
(see page 24)
1 quantity Choux Pastry
(see page 23)

For the caramel
200g caster sugar
3 tbsp water
Gold leaf to decorate

Essential equipment
Piping bags with 2cm plain
nozzle and a filling nozzle
2 baking sheets, greased
with butter and chilled
Large bowl filled with
ice-cold water
1 paper-label-free can
of beans, greased

This is such an impressive, show-stopping centrepiece, yet surprisingly easy to make. This version is a simple plain one, but you could flavour the crème pâtissière easily with a liqueur or other flavouring of your choice. The can of beans is used as a guide to start the croquembouche tower. Make sure it is well greased so you can easily slip it out, otherwise your guests will get a surprise. Gold leaf can be tricky to place as it is so statically charged. I find it best to avoid touching it with your fingers; use a small paint brush or two knives to apply it instead.

1 Preheat the oven to 220°C/Gas 7.

2 Make the crème pâtissière according to the recipe on page 24. Spread on a plate and cover the surface directly with cling film. Allow to cool completely.

3 Make the choux pastry according to the recipe on page 23 and use it to fill a piping bag fitted with a 2cm plain nozzle. Pipe small blobs of choux pastry on to the baking sheets – about 4cm across is a good size.

4 Bake for 30–40 minutes or until puffed up and golden brown. Remove from the oven and, when cool enough to handle, pierce a small hole in the base of each choux bun with a sharp knife. Place on a cooling rack to cool completely.

5 When the choux buns have cooled, beat the crème pâtissière until it is smooth and pipeable. Put it into the piping bag fitted with a filling nozzle (or simply snip the end off a disposable piping bag to create a small hole). Fill each bun with crème pâtissière.

CONTINUED OVERLEAF

CROQUEMBOUCHE
CONTINUED

6 For the caramel, put the sugar into a saucepan with the water. Stir to dissolve, then set over a high heat and do not stir again. Allow the sugar to turn a dark amber, then remove from the heat and plunge the saucepan into the ice water – it will sputter violently so do be careful. Let the caramel thicken slightly until it is viscous, and not runny. If it becomes too thick then simply place the saucepan over a very low heat to keep it in its viscous form.

7 Place the can of beans on your serving plate. Take one filled choux bun and dip it into the caramel, being extremely careful not to burn your fingers – I find it best to use a pair of heatproof serving tongs for this. Stick the choux bun on to the serving plate. Repeat with more choux buns, until you have a ring round the base of the can of beans. Repeat so that you have another ring above the first, then remove the can of beans. Repeat with the remaining choux buns, building them into a tower; you may need to hold each bun in place until the caramel sets.

8 When you have finished your tower, scoop the remaining caramel on to a fork and drizzle it all over the croquembouche. Finish with a flurry of gold leaf.

CRANBERRY, CHOCOLATE AND PECAN BISCOTTI

MAKES 18–20

125g plain flour
75g caster sugar
½ tsp baking powder
Zest of 1 orange
Zest of 1 lemon
50g dried cranberries
40g pecan nuts, roughly
  chopped
50g white chocolate chips
1 egg
1 tbsp milk

Essential equipment
Baking sheet

I used to make biscotti only at Christmastime, to give in little jars tied with a ribbon as gifts, but then I realized I was missing out. So I started to bake them for dinner parties to serve with coffee, and they go down a treat. I think the flavours of cranberry, white chocolate and pecan are spot on for this, and the colours of these ingredients actually do make it look like a work of art – maybe Hockney should worry after all.

1 Preheat the oven to 180°C/Gas 4.

2 Place the flour, sugar, baking powder, orange and lemon zest, cranberries, nuts and chocolate chips in a mixing bowl and stir together until evenly dispersed.

3 Beat the egg into the milk, and then pour this into the bowl with the other ingredients. Bring everything together into a dough – I find it easiest to use my hands. Knead it gently for a minute to bring it completely together.

4 Take the dough out of the mixing bowl and roll into a fat sausage about 23cm long. Put it on the baking sheet. (No need to line the sheet; that can make the biscuits soggy.) Bake for 25 minutes, until just golden.

5 Remove from the oven and slice into 1cm-thick pieces – a really sharp, serrated knife is best, and you need to do it gently so the biscotti sausage doesn't crumble. Place these slices back on the baking sheet and return to the oven. Immediately turn the oven down to 130°C/Gas ½, then bake for 15 minutes.

6 Allow to cool completely, and you have a batch of beautifully baked biscotti.

GATEAU AFFOGATO
SERVES 8–12

For the sponge
280g plain flour
1 tsp baking powder
1½ tsp salt
100g skinless hazelnuts,
   gently crushed
250g caster sugar
180ml water
120ml sunflower oil
2 tsp Camp coffee essence
1 tsp vanilla extract
6 eggs, separated

For the syrup
150g caster sugar
150ml water
1 tbsp Camp coffee essence
2 tbsp Frangelico liqueur

For the filling
1 litre best quality vanilla
   ice cream
3 tbsp Frangelico liqueur

Essential equipment
23cm/9-inch springform cake
   tin (do not grease or line it)
Food processor (if you don't
   have one, remove the ice
   cream from the freezer to
   soften it before starting
   the recipe)
Cling film
Pastry brush

Affogato is traditional in most Italian regions. A shot of freshly brewed espresso is poured over a ball of vanilla ice cream so that the ice cream slowly melts into the bitter coffee (affogato means 'drowned'). It is one of my favourite after-dinner treats, but I also wanted to make it into something more: something with the traditional flavours, but a little more indulgence. This frozen treat is composed of three layers of coffee and hazelnut sponge, and two layers of vanilla ice cream, and is finished with a hot coffee and Frangelico sauce syrup.

1 Preheat the oven to 150°C/Gas 2.

2 Place the flour, baking powder, salt, hazelnuts and sugar in a bowl. Slowly pour in the water and sunflower oil, mixing with a wooden spoon as you do. Add the Camp coffee and vanilla, and the egg yolks. Beat well to a smooth batter.

3 In a separate bowl whisk the egg whites to stiff peaks, then slowly fold into the batter, taking care not to lose any air. When the whites are well incorporated, carefully pour the batter into the springform tin.

4 Bake for 40–50 minutes, or until a skewer inserted into the centre comes out clean. When the cake is baked, turn the tin upside down on a cooling rack and allow to cool for 30 minutes (this is why you mustn't grease the tin – so the cake doesn't fall out).

5 To make the syrup, place the sugar, water and Camp coffee in a small saucepan, bring to the boil and allow to boil for 4 minutes. Remove from the heat and stir in the Frangelico.

6 To prepare the filling, scoop the ice cream into a food processor with the liqueur, then pulse until the ice cream is softened but not melted. If you don't have a food processor, use softened ice cream and beat in the liqueur with a wooden spoon.

7 When the cake is cooled, remove it from the tin, using a palette knife to release the sides. Slice it into 3 discs of roughly equal depth.

8 Line the tin with cling film. Place the disc of cake that was the domed top dome-down in the tin. Pour over about 3 tablespoons of the syrup and brush on with a pastry brush. Scoop half of the ice cream over this first layer of sponge, then top with the middle layer of sponge. Soak that too in 3 tablespoons of syrup, then top with the remaining ice cream and finish with the last disc of sponge, placed so that the flat bottom is now gateau top. Soak that liberally in about 4 tablespoons of syrup, then place in the freezer for 1 hour, or until ready to serve.

9 Remove the cake with the help of the cling film lining, then transfer to a serving dish.

10 Heat the remaining syrup, and pour it hot over slices of the gorgeous gateau.

HELLFIRE AND BRIMSTONE CAKE
SERVES 12–16

For the cake
9 eggs, separated
230ml water
450g caster sugar
Seeds from 2 vanilla pods, or
  2 tsp vanilla paste or extract
1½ tsp salt
160ml sunflower oil
330g plain flour
50g cocoa powder

For the ganache
400g milk chocolate
200g dark chocolate
300ml double cream
50g unsalted butter

For the honeycomb
75g unsalted butter
200g caster sugar
75g golden syrup
2 tsp bicarbonate of soda

For the chocolate spikes
300g dark chocolate
Gold leaf

Essential equipment
28cm/11-inch loose-bottomed
  cake tin (do not grease it)
2 baking sheets lined with
  baking paper
Piping bag fitted with
  large star nozzle

When I was little, I was obsessed with witches and all things spooky, so much so that I used to scare myself reading horror stories. A part of me still loves this kind of thrill, and this cake is tribute to that. It is a chocolate chiffon cake filled with ganache and honeycomb 'brimstone', finished with shards of dark chocolate.

1 Preheat the oven to 150°C/Gas 2.

2 Place the egg whites in a metal mixing bowl and set to one side until needed.

3 Place the egg yolks in a second mixing bowl and add the water, sugar, vanilla, salt and sunflower oil. Whisk together for a minute until everything is perfectly incorporated, then sift in the flour and cocoa powder and beat to a smooth batter.

4 Whisk the egg whites to stiff peaks, then beat one quarter into the cake mixture to slacken it. Place the remaining egg whites on the batter and fold in very gently. Pour into the ungreased cake tin and tap on the worktop a few times to expel large air bubbles.

5 Bake for 1 hour and 15 minutes, or until a skewer inserted into the centre comes out clean, and the cake is springy when touched. Remove from the oven and turn the tin upside down on a cooling rack. This is so the cake doesn't crush itself and go soggy when cooling, and is why you must not grease the tin – otherwise the cake could fall out.

6 Meanwhile, make the ganache by breaking the two chocolates into bits and placing in a heatproof bowl.

CONTINUED OVERLEAF

Put the cream and butter into a saucepan and warm gently over a medium heat until the butter has melted into the cream, and the mixture is hot enough that you can't keep your finger in it for longer than a second or two. Pour this over the broken chocolate, then stir together until the chocolate has melted and you have a smooth glossy ganache.

7 For the honeycomb, place the butter, sugar and syrup in a saucepan over a high heat. Allow the mixture to bubble until it goes golden brown, swirling the pan every now and again to ensure an even colouring, but don't stir or it will crystallize. This takes about 5 minutes. Once the mixture is golden brown, remove from the heat and stir in the bicarbonate, which will cause the mixture to bubble up. Quickly pour this on to one of the lined baking sheets and allow to set completely.

8 To make the dark chocolate spikes, melt the chocolate gently in a heatproof bowl over a pan of barely simmering water. Spread evenly over the baking paper on the other baking sheet and allow to set. You can cheat and pop it in the fridge if needs be.

9 Once the cake has cooled, loosen it from the tin by sliding a palette knife around the edge, then release it. Slice it in half. Put one half on a cake plate and spread with one third of the ganache. Chop the honeycomb into small shards and sprinkle this on the ganache, reserving some for the top. Top with the second layer of cake and spread the remaining ganache over the top and sides, reserving some for the piped spikes. Break the set chocolate into shards and stick around the edges of the cake. Finish with a sprinkling of honeycomb and gold leaf, and pipe the remaining ganache in spikes around the base of the cake.

CARAMEL SHARD COOKIES
MAKES 20

For the caramel
100g caster sugar
3 tbsp water

For the cookie dough
200g light brown
    muscovado sugar
150g salted butter, at room
    temperature
200g plain flour
1 tsp baking powder
Seeds from 1 vanilla pod, or
    1 tsp vanilla paste or extract

Essential equipment
1 large or 2 small
    baking sheets

These cookies were born when I was first teaching myself how to make caramel. I found I had panfuls of the gorgeous stuff going to waste, so I decided to bake it into cookies. The cookie itself is chewy and toothsome, while the caramel adds crunchiness and sweetness. I love these dipped in my hot chocolate or coffee.

1 Place the sugar and water in a pan and stir to mix them, then place the pan over a high heat and allow to boil without stirring it again. After about 5 minutes the sugar will have turned amber in colour and the bubbles will have reduced in size. Pour on to a baking sheet and leave to solidify for at least 10 minutes.

2 To make the cookie dough, beat the sugar and butter together until paler in colour and lighter in texture. You could do this with an electric whisk or in a freestanding electric mixer. Add the remaining ingredients and mix by hand into a stiff dough. Leave in the bowl and place to one side.

3 Break the dried caramel into small shards and add to the cookie dough. Stir or knead the shards into the dough until they are well incorporated. Chill the dough in the fridge for 30 minutes.

4 Preheat the oven to 170°C/Gas 3.

5 Divide the dough into 20 and roll into little balls. Place these, spread well apart, on baking sheets. Bake for 15–20 minutes, or until the cookies are baked and have turned golden around the edges. Remove from the oven and allow to cool before gobbling up.

CHAPTER TEN

HAPPY HOUR

I have been brought up on parties. I don't mean that in such a way that you should be calling social services, but I have watched over the years as Mum has thrown hundreds of dinner and cocktail parties. My family loves an excuse for a celebration, and when we have one, we go to town on it. I used to sit on the stairs watching as Mum's friends would howl with laughter, eating beautiful food and drinking from gorgeous glasses amid mountainous cake stands. I myself now adore a party or celebration, and throw them as often as I can.

This chapter contains recipes for smaller bakes, both sweet and savoury, that would be welcome at any cocktail party. And on the topic of cocktails, well, there are a few recipes for those here, too ... If you don't have a cocktail shaker, a jam jar will do.

MUSHROOM AND PARMESAN PALMIERS

MAKES ABOUT 30

1 quantity Rough Puff Pastry
  (see page 22) or 500g shop-
  bought all-butter puff
Flour for dusting
175g chestnut mushrooms
1 small red onion
1 tsp truffle oil
½ tsp salt
½ tsp black pepper
50g Parmesan cheese,
  very finely grated

Essential equipment
Food processor
2 large or 3 small
  baking sheets

These little twirls of cheese and mushroom are strong enough in flavour to please even the most diehard of meat-eaters at a party. I think they look like elephant's ears. I serve them with a hot chilli or tomato dip.

1 Flour the work surface well and place the block of pastry on it, flouring the top of the pastry and your rolling pin. Roll the pastry out, flouring beneath it as you go, into a rectangle of around 30x25cm, about 4mm thick.

2 Place the other ingredients, except the Parmesan cheese, in a food processor and blitz into an almost gritty paste. Spread evenly over the pastry, and top with the Parmesan.

3 Roll the two longest sides in towards the centre, wrapping into tight spirals that meet in the middle. You should end up with two long cylinders, joined together on the bottom. Place this in the fridge for at least 30 minutes to chill and firm up, so that when you slice into it, the palmiers don't become misshapen.

4 Preheat the oven to 200°C/Gas 6.

5 Slice the chilled dough into 30 or so pieces, around 5mm–1cm thick. Place on baking sheets and bake for 7 minutes. Flip each palmier over and bake for a further 7 minutes, or until golden brown and puffed up. Remove from the oven and leave on the tray to cool and crisp up.

TALEGGIO AND SALSICCIA GALETTE
SERVES 20

Small knob of butter and
   a drop of oil for frying
1 large red onion,
   very finely sliced
100g fennel, very finely sliced
1 tbsp balsamic vinegar
½ tsp salt
½ tsp black pepper
1 tbsp light brown
   muscovado sugar
4 Italian salsiccia (or
   your favourite sausage)
150g yellow peppers
250g Taleggio cheese
320g (approx.) roll of all-butter
   puff pastry, thawed if frozen
Leaves from about 6 small
   sprigs of thyme
1 small egg, beaten with a
   pinch of salt, for glazing

Essential equipment
Large baking sheet lined
   with baking paper

I love everything Italian. My favourite Italian deli in Manchester sells delicious Taleggio cheese, and their salsiccia, made from tender pork and fennel seeds, is out of this world. Cut this galette into canapé-sized pieces to serve at an informal party.

1 Preheat the oven to 200°C/Gas 6.

2 Melt the butter and oil in a frying pan over medium heat. Add the onion and fennel, and allow to soften slowly for about 10 minutes. If the onion and fennel start to brown, reduce the heat. When soft, add the vinegar, salt, pepper and sugar, and caramelize for a few minutes. Remove from the heat and allow to cool.

3 Slice the salsiccia into discs 1cm thick and place in a bowl to one side. Chop the peppers into 2.5cm squares and place these to one side, too. Chop the cheese into 1cm chunks, and set aside.

4 Unroll the pastry on to the baking sheet and, using a sharp knife, score a line all the way round, 1cm in from the edge. This will act as a border and puff up around the filling. Scatter the caramelized onions and fennel evenly over the pastry, keeping the border clear, then arrange the sausage and pepper on top. Add the chunks of cheese and scatter over the thyme leaves.

5 Glaze the border with the beaten egg – using a pastry brush or your fingers – then bake the galette for about 30 minutes, or until the pastry is beautifully golden and puffed, and the sausage is cooked. Season with a little more salt and pepper if needed. Cut into 20 small pieces. This is delicious hot or cold.

QUAIL SCOTCH EGGS
MAKES 12

12 quail's eggs
2 litres sunflower oil
for deep-frying
Cranberry sauce, mustard
or mayonnaise, to serve

For the sausage meat
300g pork loin
3 rashers unsmoked
streaky bacon
2 sage leaves
3 sprigs of thyme,
leaves only
2 shallots
½ tsp smoked paprika
½ tsp salt
½ tsp black pepper
A few drops of
Worcestershire sauce

For the coating
100g plain flour
2 eggs, beaten
150g white breadcrumbs,
seasoned

Essential equipment
Food processor
Deep-fat fryer or deep
saucepan

I remember many a childhood picnic where I'd spend ages trying to sink my teeth into a giant Scotch egg. These are bite-sized, and bring a sense of nostalgic charm to any drinks party. Delicious, too.

1 Bring a pan of water to the boil, add the quail's eggs and boil for 2½ minutes. Run the pan under cold water until the water is cold, and leave the eggs in the pan to cool.

2 Make the sausage meat by putting the ingredients in a food processor and blitzing. Divide this into 12 portions. I find the best way is to flatten it into a circle on a plate and cut 12 'pizza slices' out of it.

3 Decant the flour into one shallow bowl, the eggs into another, and the breadcrumbs into a third.

4 Peel the quail's eggs – my mum's tip is to tap their bottoms and peel from there so you can get under the membrane, which helps lift off the shell.

5 Take a portion of the sausage meat and ball it up, then flatten it out into a disc in the palm of your hand. Place a quail's egg in the centre and wrap the sausage meat around it, as gently as possible. Repeat until you have 12 wrapped eggs.

6 Take a wrapped egg and roll it in the flour, then dip it into the beaten egg, then roll it in breadcrumbs so that it is completely and thickly covered. Repeat with the remaining eggs.

7 Heat the oil for deep-frying until a thermometer reads 180°C or a cube of bread sizzles when dropped in. Fry the scotch eggs for about 3½–4 minutes, or until golden brown. Remove with a slotted spoon and drain on kitchen paper. Serve with dipping pots of cranberry sauce, mustard and mayonnaise.

TINY BANANA TARTE TATINS
MAKES 12

250g caster sugar
90ml water
10g unsalted butter
Pinch of salt
About 4 large,
    very ripe bananas
320g (approx.) roll of
    all-butter puff pastry,
    thawed if frozen

To serve
150ml double cream
Seeds from 1 vanilla pod,
    or 1 tsp vanilla paste
    or extract
2 tbsp icing sugar

Essential equipment
12-hole deep muffin tray,
    lightly greased
7.5cm/3-inch cookie cutter

I had never even considered a banana tarte tatin before my baker friend made one, and now I am hooked. The caramelized banana reminds me of when my dad would make me barbecued bananas on summer evenings. This is great for any cocktail party.

1 Preheat the oven to 200°C/Gas 6.

2 Mix the caster sugar and 3 tablespoons of the water in a deep saucepan. Place over a high heat and leave it until the sugar caramelizes; don't stir. Once the sugar turns deep amber and the bubbles reduce in size, remove the pan from the heat and stir in the rest of the water (75ml), the butter and salt. It will sputter, which is why a deep pan is a good idea.

3 Divide the caramel between the 12 muffin holes.

4 Chop the bananas into 1cm-thick discs. Place 3 banana discs flat on the caramel in each muffin hole – you may need to squash them in a little bit, but this will only add to the flavour.

5 Unroll the pastry and cut out 12 discs using the cookie cutter. Place each one on top of the bananas, gently tucking the sides down. Prick a small hole in the top, then bake for 35 minutes, or until the pastry is puffed up and dark golden brown.

6 Remove from the oven and immediately prise each tart out of its hole, inverting it on a cooling rack so the bananas are on top. I find it best to use a fork, working it down the sides and scooping the tarts up from underneath. Do this quickly, before the caramel hardens and sticks the tarts to the tin. Allow to cool.

7 Meanwhile, whip the cream to soft, floppy peaks. Add the vanilla and icing sugar, and whisk again. Top each tarte tatin with a dollop of this cream, and serve.

TINY APPLE TARTE TATINS
If you prefer, make these with the more traditional apple. Peel and core 2 or 3 Granny Smith apples, chop into 5mm cubes and use instead of the banana.

PARTY PANCAKELETS
MAKES 25

2 eggs, separated
120g milk
30g butter, melted
120g plain flour
1 tsp baking powder
2 tbsp caster sugar
Sunflower oil for frying

For the topping
200g tub full-fat cream cheese
4 tbsp maple syrup
12 slices of streaky bacon,
　grilled until crispy

When I first went to New York, I was shocked to see that they ate their bacon on maple syrup-soaked pancakes. When I tried it, though, I was hooked. Salty bacon and the sweet syrup is a match made in Yankee heaven.

1 Whisk the egg yolks and milk in a mixing bowl until well combined, then add the melted butter. Sift in the flour and baking powder and mix to a smooth batter, making sure there are no lumps of flour.

2 Place the egg whites in another, clean mixing bowl and whisk to soft peaks, then add the caster sugar and whisk until fluffy – you don't need to make it as stiff as it would be if you were making meringue. Add the egg whites to the bowl containing the batter, and gently fold in.

3 Put a tablespoon of sunflower oil in a frying pan and place over a high heat until the oil begins to smoke slightly, then reduce the heat to medium-high. Spoon a tablespoon of batter per pancake into the pan and fry for 1 minute, or until lots of tiny bubbles break the surface of the pancakes, then flip over and fry for 45–60 seconds longer. Repeat until all the batter is used up. Allow the pancakes to cool.

4 To make the topping, beat the cream cheese and maple syrup together, and place a scant teaspoonful on top of each pancake. Chop the bacon into small chunks, and place a small pile of bacon on each cheese-topped pancake.

CHORIZO AND MANCHEGO MINI SCONES
MAKES 10–12

50g natural yoghurt
60ml milk
1 tsp lemon juice
125g self-raising flour
125g strong white flour,
  plus extra for dusting
1 tsp salt
5g (1 tsp) baking powder
20g caster sugar
40g salted butter
1 egg
60g cooked chorizo sausage,
  chopped into 5mm cubes
60g manchego cheese,
  chopped into 5mm cubes
1 egg, beaten with a tiny
  pinch of salt, to glaze

Essential equipment
5cm/2-inch round cookie
  cutter, plain or fluted
Baking sheet, greased

*These small, savoury scones are perfect for a party –
not only are they bite-sized, but their savoury
combination goes smashingly with boozy beverages.*

1 Preheat the oven to 220°C/Gas 7.

2 Mix together the yoghurt, milk and lemon juice,
and set aside.

3 Put the flours, salt, baking powder and sugar in a
large mixing bowl. Cube the butter and rub it in until
the mixture resembles breadcrumbs. Add the egg and
rub it through into clumpy breadcrumbs, then stir in
the cheese and chorizo.

4 Slowly add the milk mixture, mixing with a spoon
or your hands into a soft but fairly firm dough.

5 Remove from the bowl and gently push together
for about 30 seconds, before flattening out into a disc
about 1.5cm thick. Cut out scones using the floured
cookie cutter and place on the greased baking sheet.

6 Glaze the tops with beaten egg (do not glaze the
sides as this will prevent the scones from rising)
and bake for 10–12 minutes, or until golden brown
and the scones sound slightly hollow when tapped
on the base.

COCKTAILS

For me, a party just wouldn't be a party without the alchemy of cocktails. Unlike making a cake batter or bread dough, you can tweak a cocktail recipe as you go along, without running the risk of ruining the whole thing. Each of these cocktails is for one.

CHERRY BAKEWELL COLLINS PER SERVING

45ml Amaretto liqueur
30ml cherry brandy
200ml cranberry or
    pomegranate juice
Ice cubes

This is the cocktail of nostalgia, and it is so dangerously drinkable that I can, and do, drink it like it's going out of fashion.

Pour the ingredients into a cocktail shaker and add a few ice cubes. Shake vigorously, then strain into a Tom Collins glass with a few extra ice cubes and serve.

TOFFEE CHOCOLATINI PER SERVING

60ml toffee vodka
30ml crème de cacao
Ice cubes

When I'm in need of sheer indulgence, this is the glass for me.

Pour the ingredients into a cocktail shaker and add a few ice cubes. Shake vigorously, then strain into a martini glass and serve.

WATERMELON AND CUCUMBER GIN AND TONIC PER SERVING

50g fresh watermelon
50g freshly peeled
  cucumber
Ice cubes
15ml sugar syrup
  (see page 25)
30ml gin, preferably
  Hendricks
Tonic water

OK, so this isn't so much a cocktail as a regular drink, but believe me when I say that if you like gin and tonic, you will love this. I first had this flavour combination in a cocktail bar on a night out, and I was so besotted with it that I refused to go to any other bar that evening.

Put the watermelon and cucumber in a sieve over a bowl and squash with a spoon so their juices run into the bowl beneath. Put the juices in a tumbler with ice cubes, and stir in the sugar syrup and the gin. Top up with the tonic water.

BLUEBERRY FRENCH 75 PER SERVING

About 10 blueberries
15ml sugar syrup
  (see page 25)
30ml vanilla vodka
  or vodka with ½ tsp
  vanilla extract
15ml lemon juice
Ice cubes
90ml dry sparkling wine
  or Prosecco

A French 75 is one of my favourite cocktails, and I particularly love this one made with blueberries and vodka.

Put the blueberries and sugar syrup into a cocktail shaker. Using a knife or fork, mush the blueberries slightly against the side so they release some juice, but don't mash them to pulp. Add the vodka and lemon juice, with a few ice cubes, seal the shaker and shake vigorously. Strain or sift into a champagne glass, then top up with the wine or Prosecco.

ESPRESSO AND HAZELNUT MARTINI PER SERVING

30ml Frangelico liqueur
30ml coffee liqueur
30ml espresso
15ml double cream
Ice cubes

When I'm in a lazy mood, and can't seem to summon any energy, this is a cocktail that helps to promote proactivity – although too many would probably have the opposite effect ...

Pour the ingredients into a cocktail shaker with a few ice cubes. Shake vigorously, then strain into a martini glass and serve.

BLUEBERRY AND LAVENDER MOJITO
PER SERVING

7 mint leaves
30g blueberries
1 slice of lemon
30ml lavender syrup
  (see page 25)
60ml vodka
30ml freshly squeezed
  lemon juice
Ice cubes
Soda water or lemonade

Lavender is used in aromatherapy as a relaxing, calming scent. This is a cocktail to chill out to. Just sip and sigh.

Put the mint leaves into a cocktail shaker and stir with a sharp knife so the mint tears as you stir it around. Add the remaining ingredients, except the soda water or lemonade, seal the shaker and shake vigorously. Pour into a tall glass and top with soda water or lemonade.

PASSIONFRUIT MARTINI
PER SERVING

60ml passionfruit liqueur
15ml lemon juice
15ml orange juice
15ml vodka
Ice cubes
Half a passionfruit

I love the tropical taste of passionfruit. I devour them fruit by pulpy fruit. When I'm feeling totally tranquil, I love to sit quietly with a glass of this in hand, leafing through recipe books.

Pour the ingredients, except the passionfruit, into a cocktail shaker. Shake vigorously, then strain into a martini glass. Scoop the pulp from the passionfruit into the glass, and serve.

ROSE AND LYCHEE MARTINI
PER SERVING

60ml lychee liqueur
30ml vanilla vodka
30ml simple sugar syrup
  (see page 25)
Dash of lemon juice
  tsp rosewater
Ice cubes
Rose petal, to decorate

The light perfumes of rose and lychee make a romantic, sensual combination. Lychee liqueur can be bought from good spirit shops, and is also available online.

Pour the ingredients into a cocktail shaker. Shake vigorously, then strain into a martini glass and finish with a floating rose petal.

INDEX

ACKNOWLEDGEMENTS

I COULD NOT HAVE KEPT MY FEET ON THE GROUND DURING ALL OF THIS MADNESS WERE IT NOT FOR MY PARTNER, PAUL. YOU REALLY ARE SUCH A GREAT EMOTIONAL SUPPORT, AND THE BEST FRIEND I WILL EVER NEED OR WANT. THANKS TO MY WHOLE FAMILY – AND THAT INCLUDES YOU ATKINS RATBAGS AND YOU BOWRA BEAUTIES – YOU ALL MEAN THE WORLD TO ME, AND I AM SO GRATEFUL FOR ALL YOUR TAUNTS AND TEASING TO KEEP MY HEAD A REASONABLE SIZE. HOLLY – YOU ATE, YOU ADVISED AND YOU AIDED. YOUR FRIENDSHIP MEANS THE WORLD TO ME. ALEX, DAN, LYDIA, BEN, MARK, ELEANOR, AND THE REST OF THE GANG – OUR FOODIE AND FILM NIGHTS ARE SHEER BLISS, AND I HOPE WE ARE STILL DOING IT WHEN WE'RE OLD AND GREY. JANE HOLT, I STILL OWE YOU A CHEESECAKE. SUSAN CONWAY, THANK YOU FOR BEING SO LOVELY. NICK JARVIE, YOUR BRUTAL HONESTY IS ALWAYS WELCOME. I AM IMMENSELY INDEBTED TO SARAH, VICKY, BARBARA, VERO, RICHARD AND EVERYONE AT HEADLINE FOR SEDUCING ME WITH THAT ALMOST FATAL CHOCOLATE CAKE, AND FOR BEING SO PATIENT WITH ME. I COULDN'T HAVE ASKED FOR A STRONGER AND MORE SUPPORTIVE TEAM. AND THANK YOU STUART AT METROSTAR FOR HELPING ME OBTAIN SUCH AN OPPORTUNITY. MARI, I CANNOT TELL YOU HOW GRATEFUL I AM FOR YOUR CARE, ATTENTION TO DETAIL AND HELP. YOUR HARD WORK MADE ME WORK HARDER.

CRAIG AND SARAH AT DAA. YOU HELP ME MAKE ALL THE RIGHT DECISIONS, AND I JUST LOVE WORKING WITH YOU BOTH. AMANDA CONSOLE, YOUR ADVICE AND CALMNESS GOT ME THROUGH THE RUSH, THANK YOU. LARRY, MS. GRAY, SARAH AND ALL AT LE CORDON BLEU, THERE IS NOTHING I VALUE MORE THAN MY EDUCATION, THANK YOU ALL SO MUCH. ALEX, EMMA AND ALL AT SMITH & GILMOUR – YOU REALLY ARE THE BEST AND I AM SO HONOURED TO HAVE WORKED WITH YOU ON THIS BOOK. MATT RUSSELL, YOU ARE A BLOODY GENIUS AND YOUR PHOTOS ARE NOTHING SHORT OF BEAUTIFUL, CHEERS! RICHARD HARRIS, I LEARNED A GREAT DEAL FROM YOU, AND YOUR UNADULTERATED PASSION FOR FOOD IS DELICIOUS. LAST BUT CERTAINLY NOT LEAST; I AM FILLED WITH GRATITUDE FOR THOSE WHO MADE MY LIFE CHANGE SO DRAMATICALLY. PAUL, MARY, AMANDA, KIERAN, NINA, SAM, TALLULAH AND EVERYONE AT LOVE – YOU'VE CHANGED THIS LAD'S LIFE, AND I AM HUMBLED!